Third Workshop on Beyond Vision and LANguage: inTEgrating Real-world kNowledge (LANTERN 2021)

Held online due to COVID-19

Kiev, Ukraine
20 April 2021

ISBN: 978-1-7138-2962-1

Printed from e-media with permission by:

Curran Associates, Inc.
57 Morehouse Lane
Red Hook, NY 12571

Association for Computational Linguistics
209 N. Eighth Street
Stroudsburg, Pennsylvania 18360

Phone: 1-570-476-8006
Fax: 1-570-476-0860

acl@aclweb.org

Additional copies of this publication are available from:

Curran Associates, Inc.
57 Morehouse Lane
Red Hook, NY 12571 USA
Phone: 845-758-0400
Fax: 845-758-2633
Email: curran@proceedings.com
Web: www.proceedings.com

LANTERN 2021

Proceedings of the Third Workshop on Beyond Vision and LANguage: inTEgrating Real-world kNowledge (LANTERN)

April 20, 2021
Kyiv, Ukraine (Online)

Introduction

Welcome to LANTERN 2021, the Third Workshop Beyond Vision and Language: Integrating Real-World Knowledge, co-located with EACL 2021. Building on the successes of the first edition co-located with EMNLP-IJCNLP 2019 and the second edition co-located with COLING 2020, the third edition of LANTERN aims to again bring together and interconnect researchers focusing on natural language research from a multimodal perspective. In particular, the main goal of the workshop is to promote and foster research which uses machine- and deep-learning techniques to interconnect language with vision and other modalities by leveraging external knowledge. We encourage contributions which exploit very diverse sources of external knowledge like knowledge graphs, fixed and dynamic environments, cognitive and neuroscience data, etc. This results in the workshop being open to all research directions which acknowledge the importance of knowledge in acquiring, using, and evaluating language in real-world settings.

In this third edition, we called for both long and short papers. All the accepted contributions are published in these Proceedings. LANTERN 2021 received 11 submissions, all of which were double-blindly reviewed by three highly-qualified reviewers. In total, 5 papers (4 long, 1 short) were accepted to appear in the Proceedings of the workshop, with an acceptance rate of around 55% (comparable to that of the first and second edition, which was around 53% and 57%, respectively).

Contributions are representative of a broad range of current problems and approaches and include among others a novel approach to image captioning, an approach for zero-shot image classification leveraging external knowledge from Wikipedia as well as a new approach for injecting structured knowledge into vision-and-language transformer models. Such richness of approaches and perspectives is in line with the purpose of the workshop, and confirms the growing interest for the integration of external knowledge for language and vision problems.

The program of the workshop, besides 5 oral paper presentations, includes invited talks by Aida Nematzadeh, Brenden Lake, Danna Gurari, and Sebastian Riedel. The workshop received sponsorship by iDeaL SFB 1102 and HuggingFace, which sponsor a best paper award.

The LANTERN Workshop Organizers

Organizers:

Marius Mosbach, Saarland University (Germany)
Michael A. Hedderich, Saarland University (Germany)
Sandro Pezzelle, University of Amsterdam (The Netherlands)
Dietrich Klakow, Saarland University (Germany)
Marie-Francine Moens, Katholieke Universiteit Leuven (Belgium)
Zeynep Akata, University of Tübingen (Germany)

Program Committee:

Afra Alishahi, Tilburg University
Alane Suhr, Cornell University
Alessandro Suglia, Heriot-Watt University
Ashutosh Modi, IIT Kanpur
Carina Silberer, University of Stuttgart
Claudio Greco, University of Trento
David Schlangen, University of Potsdam
Hao Tan, University of North Carolina
Iacer Calixto, UvA/NYU
Jacob Goldberger, Bar Ilan
Miaoran Zhang, Saarland University
Ravi Shekhar, Queen Mary University London
Sina Zarriess, University of Jena
Somak Aditya, Microsoft Research India
Stanislav Frolov, DFKI

Invited Speaker:

Aida Nematzadeh, DeepMind
Brenden Lake, NYU & Facebook AI Research
Danna Gurari, University of Texas at Austin
Sebastian Riedel, UCL & Facebook AI Research

Table of Contents

Conference Program

The program of LANTERN 2021 consists of 4 keynotes by invited speakers and 5 contributed talks. The contributed talks will be followed by a virtual break-out session in Gather town. The full program of LANTERN 2021 can be found at `https://www.lantern.uni-saarland.de/2021/`.

The five accepted papers are:

Reasoning over Vision and Language: Exploring the Benefits of Supplemental Knowledge
Violetta Shevchenko, Damien Teney, Anthony Dick and Anton van den Hengel

Visual Grounding Strategies for Text-Only Natural Language Processing
Damien Sileo

Exploiting Image–Text Synergy for Contextual Image Captioning
Sreyasi Nag Chowdhury, Rajarshi Bhowmik, Hareesh Ravi, Gerard de Melo, Simon Razniewski and Gerhard Weikum

Large-Scale Zero-Shot Image Classification from Rich and Diverse Textual Descriptions
Sebastian Bujwid and Josephine Sullivan

What Did This Castle Look like before? Exploring Referential Relations in Naturally Occurring Multimodal Texts
Ronja Utescher and Sina Zarrieß

Reasoning over Vision and Language: Exploring the Benefits of Supplemental Knowledge

Violetta Shevchenko, Damien Teney, Anthony Dick, Anton van den Hengel
Australian Institute for Machine Learning, The University of Adelaide, Australia
{violetta.shevchenko,damien.teney,anthony.dick,anton.vandenhengel}@adelaide.edu.au

Abstract

The limits of applicability of vision-and-language models are defined by the coverage of their training data. Tasks like vision question answering (VQA) often require commonsense and factual information beyond what can be learned from task-specific datasets. This paper investigates the injection of knowledge from general-purpose knowledge bases (KBs) into vision-and-language transformers. We use an auxiliary training objective that encourages the learned representations to align with graph embeddings of matching entities in a KB. We empirically study the relevance of various KBs to multiple tasks and benchmarks. The technique brings clear benefits to knowledge-demanding question answering tasks (OK-VQA, FVQA) by capturing semantic and relational knowledge absent from existing models. More surprisingly, the technique also benefits visual reasoning tasks (NLVR2, SNLI-VE). We perform probing experiments and show that the injection of additional knowledge regularizes the space of embeddings, which improves the representation of lexical and semantic similarities. The technique is model-agnostic and can expand the applicability of any vision-and-language transformer with minimal computational overhead.

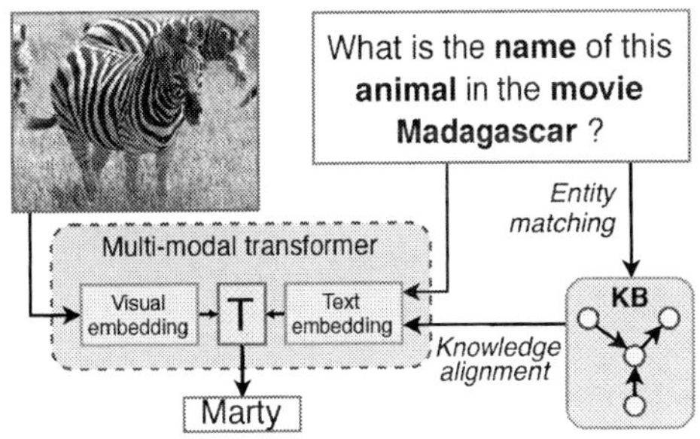

Figure 1: We inject additional information from knowledge bases (KBs) in a vision-and-language transformer. We first preprocess the KB into knowledge embeddings. When training the transformer, we use an auxiliary objective that aligns its learned representations with knowledge embeddings. In the context of visual question answering (pictured), the model is able to answer questions that require knowledge that is typically not captured in task-specific datasets.

1 Introduction

The last few years have seen a surge of interest for vision and language (V&L) tasks. These include visual question answering for example (VQA), in which the machine must answer a question about an image (Fig. 1). V&L tasks require processing two modalities and reasoning over textual, visual, and abstract concepts.

The current state of the art in V&L are models based on transformers such as BERT (Devlin et al., 2019) that have been extended to handle visual inputs (*e.g.* Tan and Bansal (2019)). These models are usually pretrained on a collection of datasets of paired textual and visual data. Suitable datasets include image captioning data (Chen et al., 2015; Sharma et al., 2018) and VQA data (Goyal et al., 2017; Hudson and Manning, 2019). Despite their large scale, these datasets only cover limited domains. Many are based on images from COCO (Lin et al., 2014) and Visual Genome (Krishna et al., 2017) and the linguistic diversity of textual annotation is limited. The V&L tasks that we are ultimately interested in require knowledge beyond current datasets, *e.g.* about specific events, named entities, common sense, and abstract concepts (see Fig. 3).

This paper focuses on the expansion of the applicability of V&L models with additional knowledge. During training, we infuse the model with knowledge from an external source, distinct from datasets of paired V&L data.The challenge is that standard V&L data is not annotated or paired with such additional knowledge. Even though techniques have

Proceedings of the Third Workshop on Beyond Vision and LANguage: inTEgrating Real-world kNowledge (LANTERN), pages 1–18
Kyiv, Ukraine (Online), April 20, 2021

been proposed to exploit additional data in NLP, including text-based question answering (Kafle et al., 2019; Lv et al., 2020; Lin et al., 2019; Rajani et al., 2019), little work has been done on the extension to V&L. Works in NLP with benchmarks of knowledge-demanding questions (Yang et al., 2015; Talmor et al., 2019; Clark et al., 2018; Mihaylov et al., 2018; Sap et al., 2019) have shown that knowledge bases (KBs) contain information that can benefit large-scale pretrained models. Motivated by this line of evidence, we aim to evaluate similar mechanisms for V&L tasks.

In the context of VQA, datasets of knowledge-demanding questions (Wang et al., 2017b; Marino et al., 2019; Shah et al., 2019) have proved challenging for existing methods. For example, a question like *Is the man eating healthy food ?* requires recognizing a type of food and relating it to its nutritional quality. Learning this type of knowledge from VQA training examples would be clearly inefficient. Other examples of challenging questions involve references to named entities such as brands, locations, or movie titles. For example, the question *Levi's is a popular brand of what item shown here ?* requires knowledge of the brand's specialization before identifying the correct element in the image. We believe that embedding this type of knowledge in a model is a necessary step to enable progress on complex multimodal question answering.

This paper describes a technique to inject information from KBs into a transformer-based model during its training (see Fig. 1). We take inspiration from Goodwin and Demner-Fushman (2019) and adapt their regularizer from text-based models to V&L transformers. We provide an implementation of our method on top of the popular LXMERT model (Tan and Bansal, 2019). We use it to investigate the suitability of several KBs to different tasks and benchmarks.

Our contributions are summarized as follows.

- We describe a method to inject information from knowledge bases during the training of vision-and-language transformers.
- We implement the method on top of the popular LXMERT model with the ConceptNet and Wikidata knowledge bases.
- We perform an extensive empirical evaluation on four downstream tasks. We demonstrate clear improvements on knowledge-demanding VQA (OK-VQA and FVQA datasets) and visual reasoning (NLVR2 and SNLI-VE datasets).
- We conduct an in-depth analysis, including ablations and probing experiments. They show that we improve the representation of lexical, semantic, and relational knowledge that is lacking in typical V&L models. This explains the surprising improvements on tasks that do not explicitly depend on external knowledge.

2 Related Work

Vision-and-language tasks require joint processing of visual and textual data *e.g.* for image captioning (Anderson et al., 2018; Hossain et al., 2019) and VQA (Wu et al., 2017; Teney et al., 2017). They have historically been approached with task-specific models, but recent transformer-based models (Vaswani et al., 2017) were shown to be applicable to a variety of tasks. A transformer can thus be pretrained on multiple datasets and then fine-tuned for one specific task (Tan and Bansal, 2019; Zhou et al., 2020; Alberti et al., 2019; Chen et al., 2020; Li et al., 2020; Lu et al., 2019; Su et al., 2019; Li et al., 2019; Sun et al., 2019). This paper describes a method to embed additional information in a transformer-based model ("additional" to the pretraining and fine-tuning datasets). Our implementation builds on the popular LXMERT model (Tan and Bansal, 2019).

Additional knowledge in NLP can help with tasks requiring commonsense or factual information (Storks et al., 2019). Various techniques have been proposed to improve transformers such as BERT (Devlin et al., 2019). Zhang et al. (2019) proposed ERNIE, which feeds graph embeddings of text entities to the model. Peters et al. (2019) proposed KnowBert, a similar technique suitable to multiple KBs. Levine et al. (2020) used WordNet to aid in the masked-word prediction objective, and improve lexical understanding in downstream tasks. Ye et al. (2019) proposed a multiple-choice question answering pretraining task and improved performance on multiple datasets requiring commonsense reasoning. Liu et al. (2020) addressed noise issues by controlling the amount of domain-specific knowledge infused into the model. Goodwin and Demner-Fushman (2019) proposed OSCAR, a regularization method to inject ontological knowledge in a pretrained language model. Wang et al. (2019) proposed to simultaneously learn knowledge representations while optimizing a masked-language objective, rather than using pretrained knowledge embeddings. All of these works were applied to NLP tasks. This paper studies the suitability of similar mechanisms to V&L tasks by applying the technique of Goodwin and Demner-Fushman (2019) to a multimodal transformer.

Knowledge-based VQA refers to benchmarks designed to require additional information (Marino et al., 2019; Shah et al., 2019; Wang et al., 2017a,b). Models have been proposed that retrieve such information from KBs based on question and image contents (Wang et al., 2017a; Wu et al., 2016a; Wang et al., 2017b; Narasimhan and Schwing, 2018). Some works use other sources of external information at training (Teney and van den Hengel, 2016) or test time (Teney and van den Hengel, 2018, 2019) but they showed limited improvements on VQA benchmarks. Recently proposed Concept-Bert (Gardères et al., 2020) model jointly learns visual, textual and knowledge embeddings to fuse commonsense information into VQA models. This paper describes a method applicable to a variety of sources of information and to tasks beyond VQA. We also show that different tasks benefit from different types of information.

3 Methodology

We describe a general, simple yet effective technique to embed additional knowledge into a transformer-based model. It is compatible with existing multimodal transformers and thus suitable to a variety of tasks. The method proceeds in three stages (see Fig. 2).

1. We preprocess the additional knowledge into a set of vector representations that we call knowledge embeddings. For example, with a relational knowledge base, we apply a graph embedding method to obtain a vector representation of every of its entities. Each is associated with a textual expression.
2. We match sentences in the V&L training data with knowledge embeddings. Matches in the training data are referred to as knowledge-rich expressions.
3. During the training of the transformer (pretraining and/or fine-tuning), we optimize an additional objective that aligns its learned representations of knowledge-rich expressions with the matching knowledge embeddings.

We now describe each stage in details.

3.1 Representations of Additional Knowledge

The versatility of the approach rests on storing the additional knowledge as a set of knowledge embeddings $\boldsymbol{V} = \{\boldsymbol{v}_i\}$ with $\boldsymbol{v}_i \in \mathbb{R}^{d_v}$. These can be produced by preprocessing sources such as text corpora (with word embedding methods) or relational knowledge bases (with a graph embedding method, see Section 4). These knowledge embeddings capture semantic information about the relations between entities, which we will incorporate into the V&L model. Each knowledge embedding $\boldsymbol{v}_i$ is associated with an instantiation $\boldsymbol{w}_i$ in the V&L data. In this work, the $\boldsymbol{w}_i$ are purely textual (single- and multiple-word expressions) but future work could consider visual representations of concepts represented by knowledge embeddings. We denote with $\boldsymbol{W} = \{\boldsymbol{w}_i\}$ the vocabulary of these instantiations.

3.2 Matching V&L Training Data with Knowledge Embeddings

We match parts of the training data with entities having additional knowledge. Since our vocabulary $\boldsymbol{W}$ contains textual expressions, we use greedy longest-string matching to identify subsequences in the data that match any $\boldsymbol{w}_i$. Possible improvements left for future work include performing named entity recognition and homonym disambiguation. In practice, entities in our KBs have unique textual representations, making homonyms a non-issue.

We represent text in the training data as a sequence of tokens $T = (t_1, ..., t_M)$. The transformer internally maps each token t_j to a word embedding $\mathbf{e}_j \in \mathbb{R}^{d_e}$. Each correspondence identified by the matching algorithm is of the form of a subsequence $(t_{a_k}, ..., t_{b_k}) \subset T$ that matches $\boldsymbol{w}_k \in \boldsymbol{W}$. We refer to such a subsequence as a *knowledge-rich expression*. To obtain a fixed-size representation $\boldsymbol{c}_k$ of a knowledge-rich expression, we sum the word embeddings of its constituent tokens *i.e.* $\boldsymbol{c}_k = \boldsymbol{e}_{a_k} + ... + \boldsymbol{e}_{b_k}$.

3.3 Aligning Learned Representations with Knowledge Embeddings

The core of the method is an additional training objective that encourages the transformer to produce representations of knowledge-rich expressions ($\boldsymbol{c}_k$) that collectively align with knowledge vectors ($\boldsymbol{v}_k$). A vector $\boldsymbol{c}_k$ as defined above is the representation learned by the model of a knowledge-rich expression. We do not expect these vectors to correspond

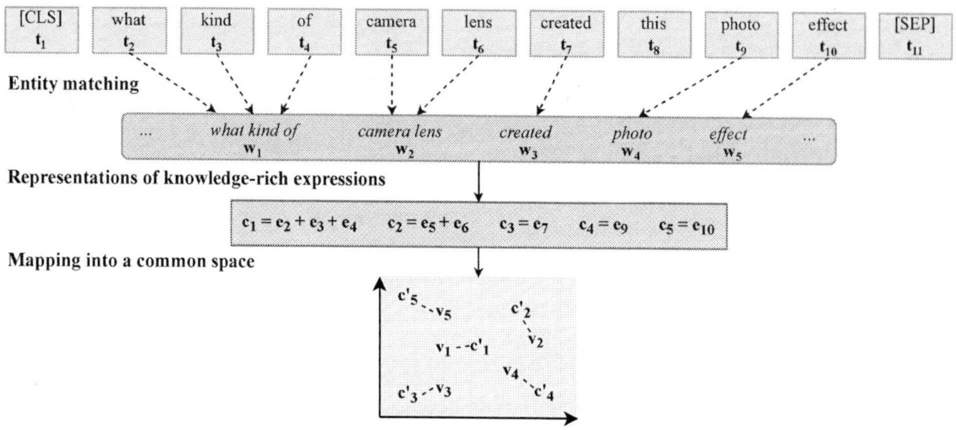

Figure 2: Summary of the approach. During training, we first match tokens in the V&L training data (yellow) with entities of the knowledge base (green). We then train the transformer with an additional loss to align the learned representations c_k (sums of word embeddings in knowledge-rich expressions from the transformer, in blue) with the knowledge embeddings v_k derived from the knowledge base.

	OK-VQA	FVQA	SNLI-VE	NLVR2
Pretraining with COCO captions, Visual Genome captions, VQA v2, GQA				
Baseline (LXMERT)	37.26 ± 0.23	52.30 ± 0.09	74.05 ± 0.19	71.31 ± 0.56
With ConceptNet PT	**39.04 ± 0.24**	54.08 ± 0.09	75.18 ± 0.21	71.61 ± 0.24
With ConceptNet FT	36.99 ± 0.01	52.19 ± 0.15	74.80 ± 0.08	70.82 ± 0.34
With ConceptNet PT+FT	38.56 ± 0.31	**54.27 ± 0.28**	**75.24 ± 0.22**	**72.59 ± 0.23**
Pretraining with VQA v2, GQA				
Baseline (LXMERT)	36.71 ± 0.22	50.38 ± 0.24	73.57 ± 0.17	67.88 ± 0.66
With ConceptNet PT	38.05 ± 0.41	51.94 ± 0.25	74.07 ± 0.48	69.47 ± 0.20
With ConceptNet FT	36.73 ± 0.50	50.54 ± 0.08	74.24 ± 0.15	67.09 ± 0.32
With ConceptNet PT+FT	38.12 ± 0.11	51.53 ± 0.17	74.26 ± 0.22	69.69 ± 0.12
With Wikidata PT	37.39 ± 0.35	51.00 ± 0.03	73.48 ± 0.17	68.27 ± 0.89
With Wikidata FT	36.31 ± 0.28	50.59 ± 0.24	73.60 ± 0.26	67.64 ± 0.19
With Wikidata PT+FT	37.43 ± 0.25	50.74 ± 0.29	73.50 ± 0.04	68.25 ± 0.51

Table 1: Overall results. Our model with ConceptNet during pretraining and fine-tuning (ConceptNet PT+FT) generally proves best. We report the average accuracy (%) ± one standard deviation over three random seeds.

to their matching knowledge embeddings $\boldsymbol{v}$, but we desire them to capture the information globally represented in the *relations* between the knowledge embeddings in $\boldsymbol{V}$. Therefore, we define a new linear layer that maps a learned representation $c_k \in \mathbb{R}^{d_e}$ to $\boldsymbol{c}'_k \in \mathbb{R}^{d_v}$:

$$\boldsymbol{c}'_k = \boldsymbol{W}_c \boldsymbol{c}_k + \boldsymbol{b}_c \quad (1)$$

where $\boldsymbol{W}_c \in \mathbb{R}^{d_e \times d_v}$ and $\boldsymbol{b}_c \in \mathbb{R}^{d_v}$ are learned weights and biases. We then define our alignment loss that encourages each projection $\boldsymbol{c}'_k$ to be close to its corresponding knowledge embedding $\boldsymbol{v}_k$:

$$L_{\text{align}} = \Sigma_k \|\boldsymbol{c}'_k - \boldsymbol{v}_k\|^2 \ . \quad (2)$$

Together, Eq. 1 and 2 encourage the global structure of the learned representations $\boldsymbol{c}$ to align with the set of knowledge embeddings $\boldsymbol{V}$ through the projection $\boldsymbol{W}_c$. The learned representations incorporate information from the knowledge embeddings while allowing the transformer to also represent task-specific information. The model is trained for the combination of its original main loss, and the new alignment loss weighted by a hyperparameter λ *i.e.* $L = L_{\text{main}} + \lambda L_{\text{align}}$.

3.4 Training Strategies

We experimented with the application of the method during pretraining and/or fine-tuning, referred to as FT, PT, and PT+FT below. Enabling the additional objective during pretraining can benefit from the larger overlap between the training data and the additional knowledge. However, most pretraining tasks do not specifically require additional knowledge, and the model may not learn to effectively use it. During fine-tuning on knowledge-demanding tasks, the model is likely to better learn to capture and use relevant additional knowledge.

3.5 Implementation

We implemented the method on top of LXMERT (Tan and Bansal, 2019), the state-of-the-art model on multiple tasks at the onset of this project. This model is pretrained on five captioning and VQA datasets: COCO and Visual Genome captions, VQA v2 (Goyal et al., 2017), GQA (Hudson and Manning, 2019) and Visual Genome QA (Zhu et al., 2016). We also include experiments with scaled-down pretraining on two datasets (VQA v2 and GQA) which will ease the computational cost of replication.

4 Experiments

We performed a suite of experiments with multiple tasks and benchmarks. Our objective is to evaluate the suitability of two popular knowledge bases (ConceptNet and Wikidata) to these tasks.

Datasets. We used four datasets. The OK-VQA (Marino et al., 2019) and FVQA (Wang et al., 2017b) are two datasets for VQA with questions that require a wide range of commonsense and factual knowledge. The SNLI-VE (Xie et al., 2019) is a dataset for visual entailment. Each instance involves an image "premise" and text "hypothesis". The task is to determine whether the image entails or contradicts the text, or whether they are neutral to each other. The NLVR2 dataset (Suhr et al., 2019) evaluates visual reasoning. Each instance is a pair of images and a text description. The task is to determine whether the text accurately describes the pair of images.

Knowledge bases. We experimented with two popular KBs. **ConceptNet** (Speer et al., 2017) is a knowledge graph that encodes the meaning of expressions useful for general language understanding. This decades-old project is built on a number of crowd-sourced and curated sources including dictionaries, encyclopedias, and ontologies. We use the 300-dimensional Numberbatch embeddings distributed by the authors of ConceptNet. They are built using the technique of retrofitting (Faruqui et al., 2015) to combine relational information from the KB with distributional semantics from word2vec (Mikolov et al., 2013), GloVe (Pennington et al., 2014), and OpenSubtitles (Tiedemann, 2012). We only use the subset of English expressions ($\sim$500,000 entities). **Wikidata** (Vrandečić and Krötzsch, 2014) is a collaboratively edited database of general knowledge. While ConceptNet mostly covers commonsense knowledge, Wikidata spans a larger domain, including historical events, celebrities, locations, science facts, *etc.* We obtain 200-dimensional embeddings with the PyTorch-BigGraph graph embedding method (Lerer et al., 2019). We use a subset of entities that have links to meaningful Wikipedia pages as done in (Wang et al., 2019). We also discard entities associated with stop words (*e.g. the, are, there*) which are common in VQA questions but carry no important semantic information. We retain $\sim$4.7M entities associated with $\sim$10M aliases.

4.1 Overall Results

We report the overall accuracy on all datasets in Table 1. Our approach clearly outperforms the baseline, with a **higher accuracy** on the knowledge-demanding VQA datasets OK-VQA (+1.78%) and FVQA (+1.97%). We also get clear improvements on the visual reasoning datasets SNLI-VE (+1.19%) and NLVR2 (+1.28%). These do not explicitly require specific knowledge, so we hypothesized that the improvement is due to the richer linguistic representations learned by our model. We verified this hypothesis through probing experiments with the SentEval toolkit (Conneau and Kiela, 2018), which showed that our model better captures multiple semantic and syntactic properties of words (*e.g.* +9.36%, +7.72%, +3.88% for word content, tense and subject number prediction respectively). We provide example results in Fig. 3.

The best training strategy is generally to use the additional objective **during both pretraining and fine-tuning** (PT+FT). Only on OK-VQA did the PT strategy perform slightly better. Comparing PT alone with FT alone (the former being superior on all datasets) shows that fine-tuning the representations is not sufficient. The additional objective induces a globally different organization of the embedding space, which cannot be reorganized during fine-tuning alone. It is also interesting to note that

	OK-VQA										
	VT	BCP	OMC	SR	CF	GHLC	PEL	PA	ST	WC	Other
Baseline (LXMERT)	34.91	29.34	35.22	46.41	40.16	32.58	32.68	35.75	**35.79**	48.68	35.96
With ConceptNet PT	**37.40**	**31.94**	37.66	**47.52**	40.82	**38.39**	**35.06**	**37.20**	31.98	48.63	**38.42**
With ConceptNet FT	34.46	29.03	35.89	46.02	39.73	33.66	32.57	35.51	35.16	45.84	35.75
With ConceptNet PT+FT	37.11	31.47	**39.06**	46.52	**40.89**	36.50	34.08	36.16	33.73	**49.56**	37.05

Table 2: Accuracy (%) on OK-VQA per question category. The method obtains clear improvements on categories related to commonsense knowledge such as **BCP**: brands, companies and products, **OMC**: objects, material and clothing, **PEL**: people and everyday life, **VT**: vehicles and transportation.

the knowledge injection during pretraining is effective despite the pretraining tasks not specifically requiring additional knowledge.

4.2 Nearest Neighbors in Embedding Space

To better understand how the regularization with additional knowledge changes the structure of the learned embedding space, we examine nearest neighbors of embeddings of individual words (see Table 3). Our model clearly captures more lexical and semantic information. For example, the nearest neighbors for *vitamin* are *calcium* and *supplements* with our model, but they are *margarita* and *amphibious* with the baseline. This stark qualitative difference was observed across the board and is not confined to cherry-picked examples. The lack of linguistic information encoded by baseline V&L transformers is unsurprising since their training data has limited linguistic diversity. Initializing a V&L model with a pretrained BERT has been proposed to address this deficiency, but it was reported to give lower downstream performance by the authors of LXMERT. In comparison, our method brings linguistic information while improving downstream performance.

4.3 Results on OK-VQA

We examine the accuracy on question categories of OK-VQA in Table 2. Each category corresponds to a type of knowledge required. We get **high gains on categories that correspond to a type of knowledge covered in ConceptNet** (objects properties and features, behavior of people, *etc.*). These include OMC (objects, material and clothing), PEL (people and everyday life), BCP (brands, companies and products) and VT (vehicles and transportation). The only category with a drop in accuracy is ST (science and technology), which is also the smallest (84 questions). The category with the largest gain is GHLC (geography, history, language, and culture), but it contains only 141 questions, and some are distant from these topics (e.g. *What fruit come from these trees ?*). These results should not be over interpreted because of the small size of these categories. Some questions also have imprecise labels. For example, the question *What activity are they doing ?* is labeled with the correct answer *video game*, and our model's answer *play video game* is considered incorrect.

The **hardest questions for our model** are those referring to exact facts and entities such as place names, famous people, or historical dates. Such precise facts are more difficult to represent and recall than "soft" commonsense knowledge. For example, the question *What year was this picture taken ?* requires to recognize a specific event and fetch a precise related fact. Other difficult questions refer to precise visual cues, while the text of the question is generic, like *What language is on the sign ?*, *Can you guess the place shown in this picture ?* or *Which season is it ?*. Recent analysis showed that V&L transformers rely primarily on the textual modality (Cao et al., 2020; Singh et al., 2020). Additional mechanisms would be needed to allow the recall of facts solely from visual cues.

4.4 ConceptNet vs Wikidata

We now examine the suitability of ConceptNet and Wikidata to the four datasets considered. **ConceptNet provides larger improvements than Wikidata on every dataset**. Wikidata shows improvements on knowledge-driven tasks (OK-VQA and FVQA) but fails to improve over the baseline on the visual reasoning ones (SNLI-VE, NLVR2). Wikidata is almost ten times larger than ConceptNet, but it contains more redundant and noisy information due to its open-source nature. ConceptNet, in contrast, is based on a collection of mostly curated sources. Finally, the vector representations of ConceptNet used were obtained through an advanced

Word	Nearest neighbors with the baseline	Nearest neighbors with our model
argentina	questioned, [PAD], neutron, dorset	argentine, uruguay, paraguay, mendoza
behaviour	[PAD], absurd, authoritative, mba	behavior, behaviors, demeanor, behavioral
bowling	boxing, smashed, dancing, 75	bowler, bowled, cricket, tennis
cottage	farmhouse, scan, condo, ##tta	cottages, bungalow, farmhouse, ##ode
facebook	jade, brady, institution, utrecht	myspace, twitter, youtube, dit
genes	[PAD], oro, subsistence, ##vah	gene, genetic, genetics, genome
lecturer	greenberg, [unused983], avoidance, ##mour	professor, prof, professors, lectures
playstation	splendid, indo, financial, tapping	xbox, wii, sega, consoles

Table 3: Examples of nearest neighbors in the space of word embeddings learned by the baseline and by our model. Our model better captures lexical and semantic similarity.

How did you make this dish?
Baseline: pasta
Proposed: boil ✓

What health benefit does this type of vegetable have?
Baseline: steam
Proposed: fiber ✓

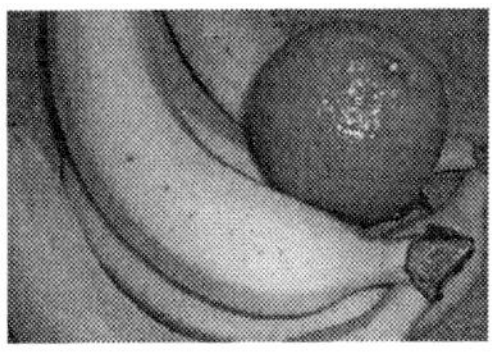

Which food in this image is full of vitamin C?
Baseline: banana
Proposed: orange ✓

Which animal is related to wolf?
Baseline: cat
Proposed: dog ✓

(a) OK-VQA. (b) FVQA.

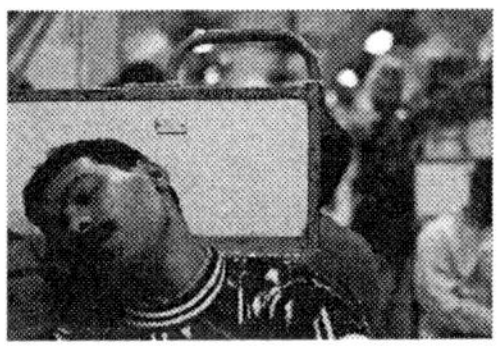

There is a man sleeping next to a woman on the subway.
Baseline: entailment
Proposed: neutral ✓

Hockey players hugging.
Baseline: entailment
Proposed: contradiction ✓

All of the bottles in the right image are unlabeled.
Baseline: false
Proposed: true ✓

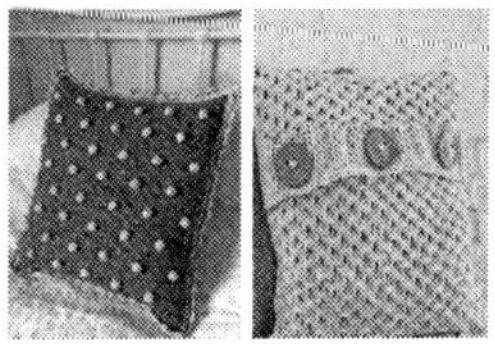

At least one of the pillows has a minimum of 4 different colors.
Baseline: true
Proposed: false ✓

(c) SNLI-VE. (d) NLVR2.

Figure 3: Test cases on which our model (Pretraining with VQA v2, GQA w/ ConceptNet PT+FT) produces better predictions than the baseline. On OK-VQA and FVQA, the questions require factual knowledge of the type found in ConceptNet. On SNLI-VE and NLVR2, the baseline frequently produces common, but incorrect answers.

and proven procedure that involves ConceptNet as well as other pretrained word representations. The representations of Wikidata used are a more direct representation of the knowledge graph.

4.5 Comparison with Existing Methods

In Table 4 we compare our results with the top entries from the leaderboards of OK-VQA[1] and NLVR2[2]. On OK-VQA, the best accuracy is shown by ConceptBert model pretrained on a captioning dataset. The other reported results are from the traditional VQA models BAN (Kim et al., 2018) and MUTAN (Ben-Younes et al., 2017). The BAN and MUTAN models supplemented with ArticleNet (Marino et al., 2019) obtain each a small improvement (+.44 and +1.43%). This component retrieves Wikipedia articles from which it extracts an answer for each question. These models perform much worse than the LXMERT baseline, which is trained on multiple datasets. We include an LXMERT model provided by its authors (LXMERT–Paper) and one retrained with code they provide (LXMERT–GitHub). The latter uses a simplified training strategy, hence a slight discrepancy (*e.g.* 69.50% on VQA v2 with their model and 68.52% with the retrained one). Our model brings a clear improvement over LXMERT-github, but it does not surpass LXMERT-paper that

[1] `https://okvqa.allenai.org`
[2] `http://lil.nlp.cornell.edu/nlvr/`

	OK-VQA	NLVR2
MLP	20.67	–
BAN	25.17	–
BAN + ArticleNet	25.61	–
MUTAN	26.41	–
MUTAN + ArticleNet	27.84	–
ConceptBert (Conceptual Cap.)	33.66	–
FiLM	–	52.1
VisualBERT (COCO captions)	–	67.00
UNITER (COCO, VG, Conceptual Cap., SBU)	–	**79.50**
LXMERT-Paper (cannot be reproduced, see text)	**42.94**	74.50
This paper: (COCO and VG captions, VQA v2, GQA, VG QA)		
LXMERT-GitHub	37.26	71.31
LXMERT-GitHub with ConceptNet	39.04	72.59

Table 4: Comparison with existing methods. Datasets used for pretraining are given in parentheses.

we could not reproduce.

On NLVR2, the classical method FiLM (Perez et al., 2018) expectedly performs worse than transformers pretrained on multiple datasets. The LXMERT baseline surpasses VisualBERT (Li et al., 2019), and our knowledge injection brings a small improvement. The state of the art on NLVR2 is obtained by UNITER (Chen et al., 2020) which is pretrained on a much greater amount of captioning data and uses a significantly larger architecture.

4.6 Knowledge Ablation

The main source of improvements on knowledge-demanding tasks like OK-VQA is the representation of knowledge relevant to test questions. To illustrate this claim, we create a small knowledge test with OK-VQA to examine how removing certain pieces of knowledge affects model performance. We select, by keyword search, a small subset of 19 test questions that focus on nutrition, on which our model obtains an accuracy of 91.11% *vs* 71.11% for the baseline. We then identify all entities related to nutrition (*e.g. health benefit, fiber, protein, vitamin, etc.*) and remove them from the knowledge base. After retraining our model with the pruned KB, the performance on nutrition questions drops markedly to 68.89%. The overall accuracy (on mostly non-nutrition-related questions) is maintained. This confirms that the withheld knowledge was indeed responsible for the high performance on related questions. The automated construction of diagnostic tests of this type could allow a quantitative evaluation and would be an interesting direction for future work.

4.7 Discussion and Limitations

Our experiments showed that KBs can expand the domain of applicability of V&L models. The tested approach proved robust in a range of settings with ConceptNet but the larger Wikidata did not fulfill our expectations. Our results suggest that the noise and ambiguities in Wikidata prevent realizing its full potential. Methods for better text-to-knowledge matching such as named entity recognition and homonym disambiguation are promising solutions to investigate.

We also identified the grounding of knowledge with visual evidence to be a limitation currently for certain tasks. Questions in OK-VQA about specific places or famous people for example require the model to recall specific facts on the basis of precise visual cues. Although such facts are stored in Wikidata, the tested model did not prove effective at recalling them. Improvements of the visual grounding could also help with visual reasoning tasks like SNLI-VE where the correct interpretation of a text input is heavily dependent on the visual input.

5 Conclusions

In this paper we described a general-purpose technique to inject external information from knowledge bases into multimodal transformers for vision-and-language tasks. The current prevailing paradigm is to pretrain large models on collections of datasets. Our experiments demonstrate that some types of commonsense and factual knowledge are not captured within these models. Knowledge bases like ConceptNet and Wikidata can fill in these deficiencies. We showed clear improvements in performance on a variety of tasks and benchmarks requiring visual and multimodal reasoning, demonstrating the versatility of the procedure.

The value of these results for future research are twofold. On the one hand, they indicate that the combination of heterogeneous sources of information is a promising way to expand the applicability of current machine learning models. On the other hand, by improving the availability of supporting knowledge, the approach opens the door to future advances on reasoning procedures that process this information. Advances on this front would lead to improved capabilities on tasks that require high-level or multi-hop reasoning, for example.

References

Chris Alberti, Jeffrey Ling, Michael Collins, and David Reitter. 2019. Fusion of detected objects in text for visual question answering. In *Proceedings of the 2019 Conference on Empirical Methods in Natural Language Processing and the 9th International Joint Conference on Natural Language Processing*, pages 2131–2140.

Peter Anderson, Xiaodong He, Chris Buehler, Damien Teney, Mark Johnson, Stephen Gould, and Lei Zhang. 2018. Bottom-up and top-down attention for image captioning and visual question answering. In *Proceedings of the IEEE Conference on Computer Vision and Pattern Recognition*, volume 3, page 6.

Hedi Ben-Younes, Rémi Cadene, Matthieu Cord, and Nicolas Thome. 2017. Mutan: Multimodal tucker fusion for visual question answering. In *Proceedings of the IEEE/CVF International Conference on Computer Vision*, pages 2612–2620.

Samuel R Bowman, Gabor Angeli, Christopher Potts, and Christopher D Manning. 2015. A large annotated corpus for learning natural language inference. In *Proceedings of the Conference on Empirical Methods in Natural Language Processing*.

Jize Cao, Zhe Gan, Yu Cheng, Licheng Yu, Yen-Chun Chen, and Jingjing Liu. 2020. Behind the scene: Revealing the secrets of pre-trained vision-and-language models. In *Proceedings of the European Conference on Computer Vision*, pages 565–580. Springer.

Xinlei Chen, Hao Fang, Tsung-Yi Lin, Ramakrishna Vedantam, Saurabh Gupta, Piotr Dollár, and C Lawrence Zitnick. 2015. Microsoft coco captions: Data collection and evaluation server. *arXiv preprint arXiv:1504.00325*.

Yen-Chun Chen, Linjie Li, Licheng Yu, Ahmed El Kholy, Faisal Ahmed, Zhe Gan, Yu Cheng, and Jingjing Liu. 2020. Uniter: Universal image-text representation learning. In *Proceedings of the European Conference on Computer Vision*.

Peter Clark, Isaac Cowhey, Oren Etzioni, Tushar Khot, Ashish Sabharwal, Carissa Schoenick, and Oyvind Tafjord. 2018. Think you have solved question answering? Try arc, the ai2 reasoning challenge. *arXiv preprint arXiv:1803.05457*.

Alexis Conneau and Douwe Kiela. 2018. Senteval: An evaluation toolkit for universal sentence representations. In *Proceedings of the Eleventh International Conference on Language Resources and Evaluation (LREC)*.

Alexis Conneau, Germán Kruszewski, Guillaume Lample, Loïc Barrault, and Marco Baroni. 2018. What you can cram into a single vector: Probing sentence embeddings for linguistic properties. In *Proceedings of the 56th Annual Meeting of the Association for Computational Linguistics (Volume 1: Long Papers)*, pages 2126–2136.

Jacob Devlin, Ming-Wei Chang, Kenton Lee, and Kristina Toutanova. 2019. Bert: Pre-training of deep bidirectional transformers for language understanding. In *Proceedings of the 2019 Conference of the North American Chapter of the Association for Computational Linguistics: Human Language Technologies, Volume 1 (Long and Short Papers)*, pages 4171–4186.

Manaal Faruqui, Jesse Dodge, Sujay Kumar Jauhar, Chris Dyer, Eduard Hovy, and Noah A Smith. 2015. Retrofitting word vectors to semantic lexicons. In *Proceedings of the 2015 Conference of the North American Chapter of the Association for Computational Linguistics: Human Language Technologies*, pages 1606–1615.

François Gardères, Maryam Ziaeefard, Baptiste Abeloos, and Freddy Lecue. 2020. Conceptbert: Concept-aware representation for visual question answering. In *Proceedings of the 2020 Conference on Empirical Methods in Natural Language Processing: Findings*, pages 489–498.

Travis R. Goodwin and Dina Demner-Fushman. 2019. Bridging the knowledge gap: Enhancing question answering with world and domain knowledge. *arXiv preprint arXiv:1910.07429*.

Yash Goyal, Tejas Khot, Douglas Summers-Stay, Dhruv Batra, and Devi Parikh. 2017. Making the v in vqa matter: Elevating the role of image understanding in visual question answering. In *Proceedings of the IEEE Conference on Computer Vision and Pattern Recognition*, pages 6904–6913.

MD Zakir Hossain, Ferdous Sohel, Mohd Fairuz Shiratuddin, and Hamid Laga. 2019. A comprehensive survey of deep learning for image captioning. *ACM Computing Surveys (CSUR)*, 51(6):1–36.

Drew A Hudson and Christopher D Manning. 2019. Gqa: A new dataset for real-world visual reasoning and compositional question answering. In *Proceedings of the IEEE Conference on Computer Vision and Pattern Recognition*, pages 6700–6709.

Sabin Kafle, Nisansa de Silva, and Dejing Dou. 2019. An overview of utilizing knowledge bases in neural networks for question answering. In *2019 IEEE 20th International Conference on Information Reuse and Integration for Data Science (IRI)*, pages 326–333.

Jin-Hwa Kim, Jaehyun Jun, and Byoung-Tak Zhang. 2018. Bilinear attention networks. In *Advances in Neural Information Processing Systems*, pages 1564–1574.

Ranjay Krishna, Yuke Zhu, Oliver Groth, Justin Johnson, Kenji Hata, Joshua Kravitz, Stephanie Chen, Yannis Kalantidis, Li-Jia Li, David A Shamma, and Others. 2017. Visual genome: Connecting language and vision using crowdsourced dense image annotations. *International Journal of Computer Vision*, 123(1):32–73.

Adam Lerer, Ledell Wu, Jiajun Shen, Timothee Lacroix, Luca Wehrstedt, Abhijit Bose, and Alex Peysakhovich. 2019. PyTorch-BigGraph: A large-scale graph embedding system. In *Proceedings of the 2nd SysML Conference*, Palo Alto, CA, USA.

Yoav Levine, Barak Lenz, Or Dagan, Ori Ram, Dan Padnos, Or Sharir, Shai Shalev-Shwartz, Amnon Shashua, and Yoav Shoham. 2020. Sensebert: Driving some sense into bert. In *Proceedings of the 58th Annual Meeting of the Association for Computational Linguistics*, pages 4656–4667.

Gen Li, Nan Duan, Yuejian Fang, Ming Gong, and Daxin Jiang. 2020. Unicoder-vl: A universal encoder for vision and language by cross-modal pre-training. In *Proceedings of the AAAI Conference on Artificial Intelligence*, volume 34, pages 11336–11344.

Liunian Harold Li, Mark Yatskar, Da Yin, Cho-Jui Hsieh, and Kai-Wei Chang. 2019. Visualbert: A simple and performant baseline for vision and language. *arXiv preprint arXiv:1908.03557*.

Bill Yuchen Lin, Xinyue Chen, Jamin Chen, and Xiang Ren. 2019. Kagnet: Knowledge-aware graph networks for commonsense reasoning. In *Proceedings of the 2019 Conference on Empirical Methods in Natural Language Processing and the 9th International Joint Conference on Natural Language Processing*, pages 2822–2832.

Tsung Yi Lin, Michael Maire, Serge Belongie, James Hays, Pietro Perona, Deva Ramanan, Piotr Dollár, and C Lawrence Zitnick. 2014. Microsoft coco: Common objects in context. In *Proceedings of the European Conference on Computer Vision*, pages 740–755. Springer.

Weijie Liu, Peng Zhou, Zhe Zhao, Zhiruo Wang, Qi Ju, Haotang Deng, and Ping Wang. 2020. K-bert: Enabling language representation with knowledge graph. In *Proceedings of the AAAI Conference on Artificial Intelligence*, volume 34, pages 2901–2908.

Jiasen Lu, Dhruv Batra, Devi Parikh, and Stefan Lee. 2019. Vilbert: Pretraining task-agnostic visiolinguistic representations for vision-and-language tasks. *arXiv preprint arXiv:1908.02265*.

Shangwen Lv, Daya Guo, Jingjing Xu, Duyu Tang, Nan Duan, Ming Gong, Linjun Shou, Daxin Jiang, Guihong Cao, and Songlin Hu. 2020. Graph-based reasoning over heterogeneous external knowledge for commonsense question answering. In *Proceedings of the AAAI Conference on Artificial Intelligence*, volume 34, pages 8449–8456.

Kenneth Marino, Mohammad Rastegari, Ali Farhadi, and Roozbeh Mottaghi. 2019. OK-VQA: A visual question answering benchmark requiring external knowledge. In *Proceedings of the IEEE Conference on Computer Vision and Pattern Recognition*, pages 3195–3204.

Todor Mihaylov, Peter Clark, Tushar Khot, and Ashish Sabharwal. 2018. Can a suit of armor conduct electricity? a new dataset for open book question answering. In *Proceedings of the Conference on Empirical Methods in Natural Language Processing*, pages 2381–2391.

Tomas Mikolov, Kai Chen, Greg Corrado, and Jeffrey Dean. 2013. Efficient estimation of word representations in vector space. *arXiv preprint arXiv:1301.3781*.

Medhini Narasimhan and Alexander G. Schwing. 2018. Straight to the facts: Learning knowledge base retrieval for factual visual question answering. In *Proceedings of the European Conference on Computer Vision*, pages 451–468.

Jeffrey Pennington, Richard Socher, and Christopher Manning. 2014. Glove: Global vectors for word representation. In *Proceedings of the Conference on Empirical Methods in Natural Language Processing*, pages 1532–1543.

Ethan Perez, Florian Strub, Harm De Vries, Vincent Dumoulin, and Aaron Courville. 2018. Film: Visual reasoning with a general conditioning layer. In *Proceedings of the AAAI Conference on Artificial Intelligence*.

Matthew E Peters, Mark Neumann, Robert Logan, Roy Schwartz, Vidur Joshi, Sameer Singh, and Noah A Smith. 2019. Knowledge enhanced contextual word representations. In *Proceedings of the 2019 Conference on Empirical Methods in Natural Language Processing and the 9th International Joint Conference on Natural Language Processing*, pages 43–54.

Nazneen Fatema Rajani, Bryan McCann, Caiming Xiong, and Richard Socher. 2019. Explain yourself! leveraging language models for commonsense reasoning. In *Proceedings of the 57th Annual Meeting of the Association for Computational Linguistics*, pages 4932–4942.

Maarten Sap, Hannah Rashkin, Derek Chen, Ronan Le Bras, and Yejin Choi. 2019. Social iqa: Commonsense reasoning about social interactions. In *Proceedings of the 2019 Conference on Empirical Methods in Natural Language Processing and the 9th International Joint Conference on Natural Language Processing*, pages 4453–4463.

Sanket Shah, Anand Mishra, Naganand Yadati, and Partha Pratim Talukdar. 2019. KVQA: Knowledge-aware visual question answering. In *Proceedings of the AAAI Conference on Artificial Intelligence*.

Piyush Sharma, Nan Ding, Sebastian Goodman, and Radu Soricut. 2018. Conceptual captions: A cleaned, hypernymed, image alt-text dataset for automatic image captioning. In *Proceedings of the 56th Annual Meeting of the Association for Computational Linguistics (Volume 1: Long Papers)*, pages 2556–2565.

Amanpreet Singh, Vedanuj Goswami, and Devi Parikh. 2020. Are we pretraining it right? Digging deeper into visio-linguistic pretraining. *arXiv preprint arXiv:2004.08744*.

Robyn Speer, Joshua Chin, and Catherine Havasi. 2017. Conceptnet 5.5: An open multilingual graph of general knowledge. In *Proceedings of the AAAI Conference on Artificial Intelligence*.

Shane Storks, Qiaozi Gao, and Joyce Y Chai. 2019. Commonsense reasoning for natural language understanding: A survey of benchmarks, resources, and approaches. *arXiv preprint arXiv:1904.01172*.

Weijie Su, Xizhou Zhu, Yue Cao, Bin Li, Lewei Lu, Furu Wei, and Jifeng Dai. 2019. Vl-bert: Pre-training of generic visual-linguistic representations. In *International Conference on Learning Representations*.

Alane Suhr, Stephanie Zhou, Ally Zhang, Iris Zhang, Huajun Bai, and Yoav Artzi. 2019. A corpus for reasoning about natural language grounded in photographs. In *Proceedings of the Annual Meeting of the Association for Computational Linguistics*.

Chen Sun, Austin Myers, Carl Vondrick, Kevin Murphy, and Cordelia Schmid. 2019. Videobert: A joint model for video and language representation learning. In *Proceedings of the IEEE/CVF International Conference on Computer Vision*, pages 7464–7473.

Alon Talmor, Jonathan Herzig, Nicholas Lourie, and Jonathan Berant. 2019. Commonsenseqa: A question answering challenge targeting commonsense knowledge. In *Proceedings of the 2019 Conference of the North American Chapter of the Association for Computational Linguistics: Human Language Technologies, Volume 1 (Long and Short Papers)*, pages 4149–4158.

Hao Tan and Mohit Bansal. 2019. Lxmert: Learning cross-modality encoder representations from transformers. In *Proceedings of the 2019 Conference on Empirical Methods in Natural Language Processing and the 9th International Joint Conference on Natural Language Processing*, pages 5103–5114.

Damien Teney and Anton van den Hengel. 2016. Zero-shot visual question answering. *arXiv preprint arXiv:1611.05546*.

Damien Teney and Anton van den Hengel. 2018. Visual question answering as a meta learning task. In *Proceedings of the European Conference on Computer Vision*, pages 219–235.

Damien Teney and Anton van den Hengel. 2019. Actively seeking and learning from live data. In *Proceedings of the IEEE Conference on Computer Vision and Pattern Recognition*.

Damien Teney, Qi Wu, and Anton van den Hengel. 2017. Visual question answering: A tutorial. *IEEE Signal Processing Magazine*, 34:63–75.

Jörg Tiedemann. 2012. Parallel data, tools and interfaces in opus. In *Proceedings of the Eight International Conference on Language Resources and Evaluation (LREC'12)*, Istanbul, Turkey. European Language Resources Association (ELRA).

Ashish Vaswani, Noam Shazeer, Niki Parmar, Jakob Uszkoreit, Llion Jones, Aidan N. Gomez, Lukasz Kaiser, and Illia Polosukhin. 2017. Attention is all you need. In *Advances in Neural Information Processing Systems*, pages 5998–6008.

Denny Vrandečić and Markus Krötzsch. 2014. Wikidata: a free collaborative knowledgebase. *Communications of the ACM*, 57(10):78–85.

Peng Wang, Qi Wu, Chunhua Shen, Anthony Dick, and Anton Van Den Henge. 2017a. Explicit knowledge-based reasoning for visual question answering. In *Proceedings of the 26th International Joint Conference on Artificial Intelligence*, pages 1290–1296.

Peng Wang, Qi Wu, Chunhua Shen, Anthony Dick, and Anton van den Hengel. 2017b. Fvqa: Fact-based visual question answering. *IEEE Transactions on Pattern Analysis and Machine Intelligence*.

Xiaozhi Wang, Tianyu Gao, Zhaocheng Zhu, Zhiyuan Liu, Juanzi Li, and Jian Tang. 2019. KEPLER: A unified model for knowledge embedding and pre-trained language representation. *arXiv preprint arXiv:1911.06136*.

Qi Wu, Damien Teney, Peng Wang, Chunhua Shen, Anthony Dick, and Anton van den Hengel. 2017. Visual question answering: A survey of methods and datasets. *Computer Vision and Image Understanding*.

Qi Wu, Peng Wang, Chunhua Shen, Anthony Dick, and Anton van den Hengel. 2016a. Ask me anything: Free-form visual question answering based on knowledge from external sources. In *Proceedings of the IEEE Conference on Computer Vision and Pattern Recognition*, pages 4622–4630.

Yonghui Wu, Mike Schuster, Zhifeng Chen, Quoc V Le, Mohammad Norouzi, Wolfgang Macherey, Maxim Krikun, Yuan Cao, Qin Gao, Klaus Macherey, et al. 2016b. Google's neural machine translation system: Bridging the gap between human and machine translation. *arXiv preprint arXiv:1609.08144*.

Ning Xie, Farley Lai, Derek Doran, and Asim Kadav. 2019. Visual entailment: A novel task for fine-grained image understanding. *arXiv preprint arXiv:1901.06706*.

Yi Yang, Wen-tau Yih, and Christopher Meek. 2015. Wikiqa: A challenge dataset for open-domain question answering. In *Proceedings of the Conference on Empirical Methods in Natural Language Processing*, pages 2013–2018.

Zhi-Xiu Ye, Qian Chen, Wen Wang, and Zhen-Hua Ling. 2019. Align, mask and select: A simple method for incorporating commonsense knowledge into language representation models. *arXiv preprint arXiv:1908.06725*.

Peter Young, Alice Lai, Micah Hodosh, and Julia Hockenmaier. 2014. From image descriptions to visual denotations: New similarity metrics for semantic inference over event descriptions. *Transactions of the Association for Computational Linguistics*, 2:67–78.

Zhengyan Zhang, Xu Han, Zhiyuan Liu, Xin Jiang, Maosong Sun, and Qun Liu. 2019. Ernie: Enhanced language representation with informative entities. In *Proceedings of the 57th Annual Meeting of the Association for Computational Linguistics*, pages 1441–1451.

Luowei Zhou, Hamid Palangi, Lei Zhang, Houdong Hu, Jason Corso, and Jianfeng Gao. 2020. Unified vision-language pre-training for image captioning and vqa. In *Proceedings of the AAAI Conference on Artificial Intelligence*, volume 34, pages 13041–13049.

Yuke Zhu, Oliver Groth, Michael Bernstein, and Li Fei-Fei. 2016. Visual7w: Grounded question answering in images. In *Proceedings of the IEEE conference on computer vision and pattern recognition*, pages 4995–5004.

Reasoning over Vision and Language: Exploring the Benefits of Supplemental Knowledge

Appendices

A Implementation Details

Most transformer-based V&L models map the input text tokens to word, segment, and position embeddings, that are ultimately combined. Our approach is applied on the word embeddings.

The implementation of our method builds on top of the official implementation of LXMERT[3] (Tan and Bansal, 2019). We use values of hyperparameters recommended in the code, including a reduced number of 12 training epochs (compared to 20 mentioned in the paper) and single-stage training strategy.

The loss weight λ was selected by cross-validation for maximum accuracy on the OK-VQA validation set. From the set $\{0.1, 0.5, 1, 10, 100, 200\}$, the optimal values were found to be 0.5 for Wikidata and 100 for ConceptNet. The optimal λ seems to vary in inverse proportion with the size of the KB (based on Wikipedia, ConceptNet, and three other KBs used in preliminary experiments and not included in the paper).

The fine-tuning experiments used the same batch size of 32 and learning rate of 0.00005 as the original LXMERT implementation. The number of fine-tuning epochs was adjusted according to the dataset size: 25 for OK-VQA and FVQA, 8 for NLVR2 and SNLI-VE.

The pretraining experiment used two NVIDIA Tesla M40 GPUs and took about four days. To pretrain the model on the full five datasets we used four GPUs and each experiment took up to eight days. The fine-tuning experiments used a single GPU and took about 1h for FVQA, 3h for OK-VQA, 10h for NLVR2, and 22h for SNLI-VE.

Since the matching of KB entities with the V&L training data proceeds by exact string matching, we processed the KB entities with the same WordPiece tokenizer (Wu et al., 2016b) as the LXMERT model does for the V&L training data. To enable fast indexing of the KB, we store the knowledge embeddings $\boldsymbol{V}$ as a hash table indexed by textual expressions $\boldsymbol{W}$.

[3] https://github.com/airsplay/lxmert

B Negative Results

We explored a variety of architectural choices, but some of them did not gain any improvement over the baseline. To measure the distance between learned projections and their embeddings in Eq. 2 we tried two other options: smooth L1 loss and cosine distance, but they showed worse results than the used mean squared error. To obtain representations for knowledge-rich expressions we first included additional knowledge embedding layer as a fourth component of textual representations along with word, segment and position embeddings. This technique proved to be inefficient, so eventually we used word embeddings as a target for knowledge alignment.

Further, we tried to leverage information about objects detected in the image. We used predicted labels for each image object as a knowledge-rich expression and added another learning objective to align visual embeddings with corresponding knowledge. With this objective the model converged to a smaller loss during pretraining but the accuracy on all fine-tuning tasks was lower than the baseline results thereby indicating possible overfitting. We think that a better way to exploit visual information would be to use object labels as additional supervision to enhance entity matching.

C Linguistic Probing Analysis

We analyzed the representations learned by our model with probing tasks using the SentEval toolkit (Conneau and Kiela, 2018). This complements the evaluation on downstream tasks presented in the main paper.

The probing tasks aim to identify the linguistic information encoded in the learned representations. Following (Cao et al., 2020), we tested our model on the following ten linguistic probing tasks (Conneau et al., 2018):

- **SentLen:** predict the length of sentences;
- **WC:** word content task requires to predict which words appear in the sentence;
- **TreeDepth:** categorize the sentence according to the depth of its syntax tree;
- **TopConst:** predict the sequence of top constituents;
- **BShift:** check whether two random adjusted words have been inverted in the sentence;

- **Tense:** predict the tense of the main-clause verb;
- **SubjNum:** predict if the main-clause subject is in singular or plural form;
- **ObjNum:** same as SubjNum but for the main-clause object;
- **SOMO:** semantic odd man count task is to determine if a random noun or verb has been replaced.
- **CoordInv**: check whether two coordinate clauses have been inverted.

These tasks are designed to evaluate the quality of sentence embeddings, but LXMERT model learns separate embeddings for each token. To obtain sentence representations, we thus take outputs of 9 intermediate layers in the language encoder and average each of them across all tokens. Every layer output is used as a separate embedding and we report the best result across all layers (Table 5). Since the first 9 layers perform attention over textual modality only, no image input is required.

The results show that our model surpasses the baseline in most of the tasks. The highest gain (+9.36%) is seen in WC category meaning that our model better captures the content of words in a sentence. Importantly, best results for this task are obtained with the first layer outputs. WC accuracy drops for every subsequent layer output til it reach 16.11% and 18.65% for the baseline and our model respectively. It implies that information about individual words is well encoded in early layers but gets washed off with further self-attention. Surprisingly, we observe a noticeable gain in accuracy for predicting tense and plurality of words (Tense, SubjNum and ObjNum). Slight improvements in BShift and CoordInv tasks may be caused by additional constrains imposed on the word order by our model where the order of tokens that constitute a knowledge-rich expression is important. Finally, SentLen and TreeDepth probes highly rely on length of sentences and since both tested models limit textual input to 20 tokens, the results may not be reliable.

D Nearest Neighbors in Embedding Space

We provide in Table 6 a random selection of words and their nearest neighbors in the space of learned embeddings. We computed these neighbors using the L2 distance. Using the cosine distance gives qualitatively similar results.

E Results on NLVR2

We examine the extended metrics on NLVR2 in Table 7. The "consistency" reflects whether the model answers a given question correctly for all related pairs of images. Our model shows a **clear improvement in consistency** over the baseline (34.65 → 37.56). This suggests that the model can better relate a given textual input to different image contexts. We also report the accuracy on the balanced and unbalanced test sets, designed to evaluate a model's reliance on visual biases. In the balanced set, every image pair appears twice, one with each label (true/false). A drop in performance from the standard test set ("All") to the balanced set ("Bal.") would indicate that the method exploits biases. Neither the baseline nor any of the described models show an undesirable reliance on image biases.

F Description of Datasets

OK-VQA (Marino et al., 2019) is an open-ended VQA dataset where all questions require some sort of outside knowledge. It comprises about 14,000 questions about images from the MS COCO (Lin et al., 2014) dataset. All questions are produced by human annotators based either on information found in Wikipedia, or commonsense knowledge and visual evidence from the images. The questions are divided into ten categories (see Table 8) according to the type of knowledge needed to answer them. OK-VQA is one of the most diverse VQA datasets currently available that requires general knowledge. We use it accordingly as a primary benchmark in this study.

FVQA (Wang et al., 2017b) is a VQA dataset that contains about 5,000 questions that probe for commonsense knowledge. The questions are produced by annotators in procedure that forces the question to involve facts found in a reference KB. Each question in the dataset is therefore associated with one specific "supporting" fact that describes a relation between concepts in the question and/or image. We do not use the annotations of these supporting-facts. FVQA provides five different training/test splits. We report results that correspond to the average across the five splits. The quality of the questions in FVQA is mediocre in comparison to OK-VQA, and it is also much smaller. We include it in this study because it previously served to evaluate other models designed to use KBs for VQA.

SNLI-VE (Xie et al., 2019) is a dataset for a vi-

	SentLen	WC	TreeDepth	TopConst	BShift	Tense	SubjNum	ObjNum	SOMO	CoordInv
Baseline	69.10 (6)	56.83 (1)	32.71 (7)	67.04 (4)	66.19 (9)	74.38 (6)	76.38 (8)	75.85 (7)	**51.01 (7)**	59.52 (6)
Ours	**70.36 (5)**	**66.19 (1)**	**33.35 (5)**	**71.49 (6)**	**68.23 (8)**	**82.10 (1)**	**80.26 (7)**	**79.02 (7)**	50.70 (5)	**60.24 (7)**

Table 5: Results on linguistic probing tasks. For each, we report the maximum score obtained across layers, with the corresponding layer number in parentheses. Our model (ConceptNet PT) outperforms the baseline (LXMERT) in most probing tasks.

Word	Nearest neighbors with the baseline	Nearest neighbors with our model
birth	##gm, dat, sensitive, incorporated	births, childbirth, born, newborn
boxers	dare, indo, briefs, aiding	boxer, briefs, underwear, panties
creeping	goalscorer, fertility, ineffective, [PAD]	crept, creep, crawling, sneaking
dependent	bacterial, [PAD], ##idad, outlaws	depended, depend, depends, dependency
displaced	neptune, roche, peterborough, norway	displacement, refugees, relocated, atletico
down	up, MASK, ##combe, ##ending	up, on, out, ##s
equity	[PAD], implementations, eurasian, newfound	investors, investments, investor, investment
ghosts	[PAD], germain, combustion, ##ignment	ghost, ghostly, haunted, phantom
indication	neptune, musee, converting, legion	indications, indicating, signaled, indicative
limb	stump, branch, limbs, thorn	limbs, branch, leg, ##wara
policemen	cowboys, firefighters, youths, 37	policeman, police, cops, constabulary
quebec	sutton, [PAD], monasteries, frederick	montreal, laval, ontario, sudbury
smells	[PAD], aiding, preston, quentin	smelled, smell, odor, scent
successes	[PAD], kilometres, tina, marne	success, achievements, accomplishments, successful
sugar	yeast, powder, memo, coating	chocolate, butter, candy, celaena
taste	feel, smell, fade, become	tastes, flavor, tasted, flavors
unmarried	[PAD], [unused285], [unused685], ##dium	divorced, childless, widowed, marrying
vintage	retro, antique, victorian, rustic	antique, retro, old, ##60

Table 6: Selection of words and four nearest neighbors in the space of word embeddings learned by the LXMERT baseline and our model. The embedding space of our model better reflects lexical and semantic similarity.

sual entailment task. The task is an extension of the classical task of natural language inference (NLI). The visual version involves an image "premise" and a text "hypothesis". The model must determine whether the hypothesis contradicts the information shown in the image, entails it, or whether there are not enough clues to draw any conclusion. The SNLI-VE dataset contains about 560,000 instances, which were constructed from captions from SNLI (Bowman et al., 2015) paired with images from Flickr30k (Young et al., 2014). Despite similarities in the skills required for this task and for VQA, existing VQA models show relatively poor performance on SNLI-VE. The authors of the dataset attribute it to the need for more fine-grained visual understanding and reasoning, and they suggested the use of external knowledge to improve performance, hence its inclusion in this study.

	NLVR2 Test-P			
	All	Consist.	Bal.	Unbal.
Baseline (LXMERT)	71.31	34.65	70.34	72.45
With ConceptNet PT	71.61	34.84	71.11	72.60
With ConceptNet FT	70.82	34.42	69.86	72.35
With ConceptNet PT+FT	**72.59**	**37.56**	**72.12**	**73.71**

Table 7: Detailed metrics on NLVR2: consistency (%) and accuracy (%) on balanced and unbalanced subsets. The method brings a clear improvement in consistency.

NLVR2 (Suhr et al., 2019) is a dataset that evaluates visual reasoning over pairs of images. Each of the ~107,000 instances in the dataset consists of two images with a statement in natural language. The model must predict whether the statement accurately describes the pair of images. The creation of the dataset emphasized the linguistic diversity of the sentences, with the objective for the task to require some compositional reasoning. We use this task in our study to evaluate the suitability of our model to perform compositional reasoning on the knowledge injected in them from KBs.

Alias	Category	Example
VT	Vehicles and Transportation	What is the title of the person driving this vehicle ?
BCP	Brands, Companies and Products	Name the laptop model shown in this picture ?
OMC	Objects, Material and Clothing	What sort of room is this woman sitting in ?
SR	Sports and Recreation	What is this baseball player doing ?
CF	Cooking and Food	Which of the foods here have the highest saturated fats ?
GHLC	Geography, History, Language and Culture	What city is this meeting taking place ?
PEL	People and Everyday Life	What kind of hairstyle does the woman in the black shirt have ?
PA	Plants and Animals	What sound does this animal make ?
ST	Science and Technology	Which rodent has a similar name to the technical device seen ?
WC	Weather and Climate	What kind of clouds are shown ?

Table 8: Categories of questions in the OK-VQA dataset corresponding to the type of knowledge required.

	Images	Questions	Answers	Type
OK-VQA	14,031	14,055	14,456	knowledge-based VQA
FVQA	2,190	5,826	954	knowledge-based VQA
SNLI-VE	31,783	565,286	3	entailment
NLVR2	141,480	107,292	2	reasoning

Table 9: Summary of datasets used in the experiments.

G Additional Qualitative Results

What are they riding on?
Baseline: ski ✓
Proposed: ski ✓
GT: ski, snowboard

What is outside of the window?
Baseline: pane
Proposed: tree ✓
GT: bench, tree, table

What is the blue eagle on the buffet made out of?
Baseline: metal
Proposed: plastic
GT: ice

What type of business is this picture taken in?
Baseline: hotel ✓
Proposed: hotel ✓
GT: hotel

What season are these gourds typically harvested in?
Baseline: fall ✓
Proposed: summer
GT: fall

What is the man in that ad riding?
Baseline: ski
Proposed: snowboard ✓
GT: snowboard, microphon, board

How many chromosomes do these creatures have?
Baseline: 3
Proposed: 46 ✓
GT: 46, 23 pair, 23

What website is the left computer currently on?
Baseline: flickr
Proposed: flickr
GT: googl, weathergov, yahoocom, amazon

(a) OK-VQA.

What is the large object in the right of this image used for?
Baseline: tennis
Proposed: playing tennis
GT: play tennis

Where can people find fish?
Baseline: fish
Proposed: fish
GT: lakes rivers and ocean

What is the brass object in this image?
Baseline: cello
Proposed: trombone ✓
GT: trombone

What the woman is using to insert screw?
Baseline: toothbrush
Proposed: screwdriver ✓
GT: screwdriver

Which kind of outdoor recreation are shown in this image?
Baseline: skis ✓
Proposed: skis ✓
GT: skis

Which object in this image is used for sitting?
Baseline: couch
Proposed: couch
GT: sofa

Which objects in this image may be known as avians?
Baseline: boats
Proposed: bird
GT: birds

What object in this image is commonly eaten for lunch?
Baseline: sandwich ✓
Proposed: sandwich ✓
GT: sandwich

(b) FVQA.

Figure 4: Random selection of test instances from OK-VQA and FVQA datasets, with predictions of the baseline (LXMERT) and of our model (Pretraining with VQA v2, GQA w/ ConceptNet PT+FT).

A man plays violin.
Baseline: contradiction
Proposed: entailment ✓
GT: entailment

There are many children.
Baseline: entailment ✓
Proposed: entailment ✓
GT: entailment

A group of casually dressed people stand in the room.
Baseline: contradiction ✓
Proposed: contradiction ✓
GT: contradiction

The boy is wearing overalls.
Baseline: contradiction
Proposed: neutral ✓
GT: neutral

A man plays with a dog.
Baseline: entailment ✓
Proposed: contradiction
GT: entailment

A cat sleeps indoors.
Baseline: contradiction ✓
Proposed: contradiction ✓
GT: contradiction

The man is cutting steak on the counter.
Baseline: contradiction ✓
Proposed: contradiction ✓
GT: contradiction

The Broadway Rite Aid captures the attention of everyone who walks by due to the good sales.
Baseline: neutral ✓
Proposed: neutral ✓
GT: neutral

(a) SNLI-VE.

An image shows a forward-facing non-standing hound with a paw on some type of toy.
Baseline: true ✓
Proposed: false
GT: true

At least one image is of a multi-serving trifle bowl.
Baseline: false ✓
Proposed: false ✓
GT: false

One of the images features exactly three musicians.
Baseline: false
Proposed: false
GT: true

An image shows exactly one fragrance bottle displayed on the right of an upright black box.
Baseline: false
Proposed: true ✓
GT: true

All the instruments are standing on their ends.
Baseline: true
Proposed: false ✓
GT: false

A beetle on top of a dungball is facing left.
Baseline: true
Proposed: false ✓
GT: false

There is a plant near the cabinet in the image on the left.
Baseline: true ✓
Proposed: true ✓
GT: true

Each sled driver is driving a group of at least five dogs.
Baseline: false ✓
Proposed: false ✓
GT: false

(b) NLVR2.

Figure 5: Random selection of test instances from SNLI-VE and NLVR2 datasets, with predictions of the baseline (LXMERT) and of our model (Pretraining with VQA v2, GQA w/ ConceptNet PT+FT).

Visual Grounding Strategies for Text-Only Natural Language Processing

Damien Sileo

Department of Computer Science (CS)
KU Leuven
damien.sileo@kuleuven.be

Abstract

Visual grounding is a promising path toward more robust and accurate Natural Language Processing (NLP) models. Many multimodal extensions of BERT (e.g., VideoBERT, LXMERT, VL-BERT) allow a joint modeling of texts and images that lead to state-of-the-art results on multimodal tasks such as Visual Question Answering. Here, we leverage multimodal modeling for purely textual tasks (language modeling and classification) with the expectation that the multimodal pretraining provides a grounding that can improve text processing accuracy. We propose possible strategies in this respect. A first type of strategy, referred to as *transferred grounding* consists in applying multimodal models to text-only tasks using a placeholder to replace image input. The second one, which we call *associative grounding*, harnesses image retrieval to match texts with related images during both pretraining and text-only downstream tasks. We draw further distinctions into both strategies and then compare them according to their impact on language modeling and commonsense-related downstream tasks, showing improvement over text-only baselines.

1 Introduction

Representation of text with transferable encoding is a central task of artificial intelligence. Transfer from larger and larger transformer-based text encoders trained on masked language modeling has become a standard way to achieve state-of-the-art results. Progress is shown in tasks such as natural language inference and semantic similarity estimation when evaluated on natural language understanding benchmark datasets (Kaplan et al., 2020) such as GLUE and SuperGLUE (Wang et al., 2019). However, these scores do not tell the whole story. Firstly, marginally better benchmark scores can come at the price of impractical GPU requirements. Secondly, super-human scores can be obtained by exploiting spurious dataset-specific correlations instead of more generalizable reasoning (Niven and Kao, 2019). Mastering commonsense reasoning is regarded as a requirement for "true" language understanding (Bisk et al., 2020), and grounding representations of natural language on other modalities such a visual perception is a privileged strategy in that endeavor. Since the meaning of language stems from the physical world, visual grounding[1] is a valuable way to guide the training of NLP models. Thus, we hypothesize that text encoders, even already pretrained on a massive amount of text-only data, can be improved by a further multimodal pretraining stage.

Many visuolinguistic transformer architectures such as LXMERT (Tan and Bansal, 2019) VilBERT (Lu et al., 2019) or VL-BERT (Su et al., 2019) have been proposed to augment BERT (Devlin et al., 2019) with joint text-image understanding in order to tackle multimodal tasks including visual question answering and image retrieval, each leading to substantial performance improvement over the previous state of the art. To that end, these models generalize BERT's Masked Language Modeling (MLM) objective to a multimodal setting. More specifically, they perform the MLM task on image captions while allowing the model to use features of the paired image[2], and also perform image modeling while letting the model attend to textual features. Nevertheless, it is not clear whether joint pretraining is better than text-only pretraining when transferring to text-only tasks (e.g., language modeling, text classification, similarity estimation) and how it should be done. In this work, we address this question by breaking down the strategies toward

[1] Here, we define visual grounding as learning language representations from explicit visual associations.

[2] An image is represented as a sequence of regions features extracted with a Convolutional Neural Network.

Proceedings of the Third Workshop on Beyond Vision and LANguage: inTEgrating Real-world kNowledge (LANTERN), pages 19–29
Kyiv, Ukraine (Online), April 20, 2021

that endeavor.

A first proposed way to leverage visuolinguistic models for textual tasks is to perform the aforementioned joint modeling pretraining and then fine-tuning on text-only tasks while using a placeholder as image input. However, this only trains the text encoder on the caption domain (which is different from the wider domain usually used to train text encoders) and the model is not exposed to any training example without images. To alleviate this problem, it is possible to combine joint masked modeling on captioned images with unimodal MLM on a broader domain text-only corpus during pretraining by associating an image placeholder with the text-only examples. We call this strategy *transferred grounding*.

We also propose another technique named *associative* grounding where for each textual input, an association module retrieves the most relevant images from a large external images collection. The text encoder parameters can then harness these externally provided images for better text understanding instead of having to internally model them.

Since we are bringing an additional computational cost by using images and not only pure text, we will strive to reduce the incurred additional memory usage in our models.

The goal of this paper is to identify and compare techniques that bridge visuolinguistic multimodal modeling with text-only tasks. To that aim, our contributions are the following: (i) 4 visuolinguistic grounding strategies for text-only tasks transfer; (ii) An evaluation of the size/accuracy trade-off of image representation to reduce the memory usage of multimodal transformers; and (iii) A systematic comparison of the proposed strategies for transformers on English text-only tasks.

2 Grounding strategies

In this section we present the two main grounding strategies, that is *transferred grounding* and *associative grounding*, of which Figure 1 shows an overview. We first describe the multimodal model architecture used in both grounding strategies.

2.1 Multimodal model structure

We rely on a setup shared by several multimodal extensions of BERT (Tan and Bansal, 2019; Su et al., 2019; Lu et al., 2019). The text encoding takes place in two stages. The output of the text unimodal encoder (e.g., BERT) provides an intermediate rep-

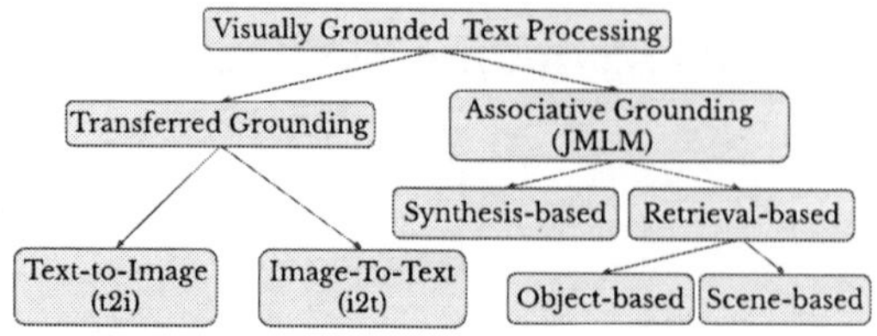

Figure 1: A categorization of the proposed grounding strategies.

resentation of the text input. The visual input has a vector representation (typically CNN-extracted embedding possibly contextualized with a transformer model). Then, both are fed to a cross-modal encoder that learns to compose the modalities in order to perform visuolinguistic modeling tasks. This multimodal model structure is illustrated in both Figures 2 and 3.

This architecture could directly be used in order to perform downstream tasks. However, a multimodal pretraining, for instance through masked modeling, is key to achieve high performance (Tan and Bansal, 2019).

2.2 Masked modeling of multimodal features

In our grounding strategies we rely on masking. In Joint Masked Language Modeling (JMLM), random tokens of the input text t are replaced by a [masked] token. A softmax JMLM head on top of the cross-modal encoder has to predict the original value of the masked tokens through cross-entropy (H) loss minimization. The cross modal encoder is thus incentivized to use the visual input regions r when they are relevant for the masked tokens prediction. Joint Masked Region Modeling (JMRM) is the visual counterpart of JMLM. Here, image region features are masked and have to be predicted, for example, through a L_p loss minimization, based on both the text and non-masked visual cues. The corresponding losses are the following:

$$\mathcal{L}_{\text{JMLM}} = \sum_{k=1}^{|t|} m_k \mathrm{H}(t_k, \hat{t}_k(\bar{t}, r))$$

$$\mathcal{L}_{\text{JMRM}} = \sum_{k=1}^{|r|} m_k \mathrm{L}_p(r_k, \hat{r}_k(t, \bar{r}))$$

where $m_k = 1$ when a token/region is masked, $\bar{t}/\bar{r}$ represents the masked tokens/regions sequence, $\hat{t}$ the predicted probability distributions, and $\hat{r}$ the predicted region features.

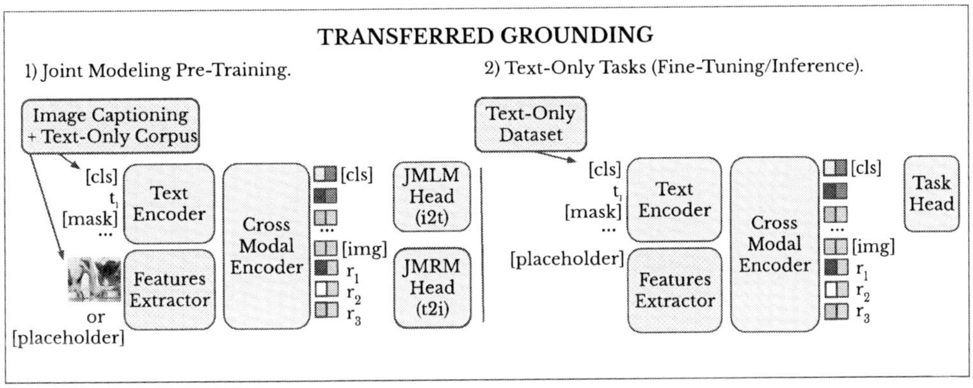

Figure 2: Overview of the Transferred grounding strategy.

2.3 Transferred grounding

In *transferred grounding* the masked modeling of multimodal features is used in pretraining as shown in Figure 2.

The corpus used for pretraining contains images paired with captions, which can also be extended with another text-only corpus. Adding examples from a text-only corpus allows the encoder to be exposed to a wider domain of text during pretraining. Since no image is available for these examples, we replace the image features by a single trainable embedding $h_{\text{[placeholder]}} \in \mathbb{R}^d$ where d is the dimension of the cross-modal encoder inputs.

Cross-modal prediction can occur in the two following directions, each providing a different way to ground language understanding.

2.3.1 Transfer from Text-To-Image prediction (t2i)

Pretraining a model to perform JMRM incentivizes the text representations to abstract the visual knowledge involved in visual region modeling. This provides a form of grounding that could be useful for textual downstream tasks. Here the model learns to predict masked image aspects from text, which might help language understanding by visually imagining the language content.

2.3.2 Transfer from Image-To-Text prediction (i2t)

A different way to perform pretraining is to perform JMLM in the presence of visual input. The model can learn to use visual information for textual modeling, thus developing useful abstractions. We hypothesize that these abstractions can help text-only tasks when the visual input they relied on is missing.

2.3.3 Text-only tasks

Once pretrained, the multimodal architecture can be applied to text-only tasks. To do so, the placeholder features $h_{\text{[placeholder]}}$ are used to replace the missing visual input.

2.4 Associative Grounding

In an alternative grounding strategy, called *associative grounding*, we do not rely on a text corpus that is a priori paired with images, but the pairing is part of the model. As seen in Figure 3, for each text input[3] t (e.g., sentence or paragraph), a visual association module retrieves the most relevant images from an archive of images.

Here, we instantiate the visual association module in the following way. A query encoder provides representation q_t for the masked input text t using the cross-modal encoder described above, and a relevance metric $\mathrm{R}(q_t,k_i)$ such as the cosine similarity identifies the K most relevant images in a collection M of images i, which are encoded into key vector representations $\{k_i, i \in M\}$.

Associated images can be visual scenes that match the input text as a whole. However, the space of situations matching the content of the input text is immense, and in many cases, the most relevant images in M will only be loosely associated to the textual input. Decomposing the situation evoked in the text into objects that play an important role can help narrowing down the space of possible relevant images, thus leading to closer associations, albeit more partial. We call the first substrategy *scene-based* and the second one *object-based.*

[3]During JMLM pretraining, the masked text is used to find associations. This to prevent trivial prediction of the masked text tokens from their presence in the images.

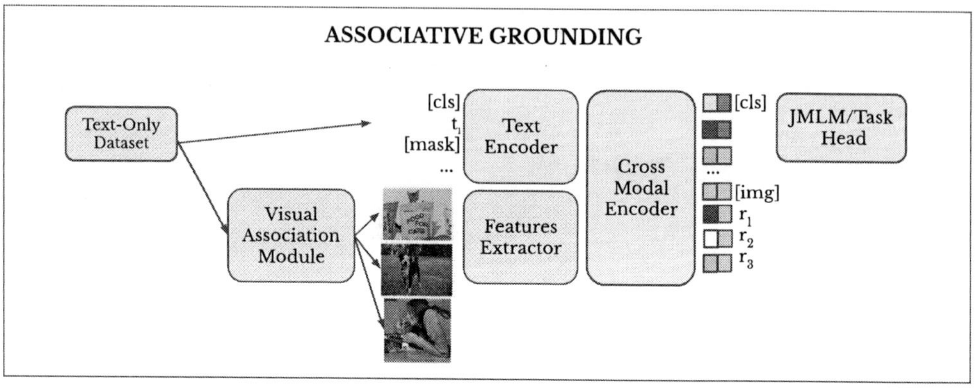

Figure 3: Overview of the Associative grounding strategy.

2.4.1 Scene-based association

Here we propose to use textual captions to index images.Each input text t is then associated with the K most similar images, according to the relevance computation of a caption given the input text. Of course, retrieved images may not be sufficiently relevant, and it is not clear whether some sentences can be illustrated by existing images. But we hypothesize that the cross-modal encoder of the captions is able to ignore non-relevant information. Kiela et al. (2014) have shown that image retrieval systems map abstract words to high dispersion results, that is, retrieved images are different to each other. This dispersion could be informative for the cross-modal encoder. Besides, concrete images could also ground more abstract concepts (Lakoff and Johnson, 1980); a very simple illustration of this is that images captioned with references to *sadness* tend to be darker than those containing the word *happiness*.

2.4.2 Object-based associations

Another possibility is to rely on objects mentioned in the text. Here, we extract all common nouns in the input text and perform a Gaussian Mixture Clustering to extract $\kappa \leq K$ clusters among the noun representations to find the key concepts. For each centroid, the closest noun is chosen as a representative. A noun-indexed database, here ImageNet22K (Deng et al., 2009), can be used to map these nouns to images.

The two association systems used in the experiments are illustrated in Figure 4 in the appendix.

2.4.3 Image synthesis

It would also be possible to synthesize images that represent the input text with a dedicated model. We experimented with the *DeepAI* system[4] and as shown in Figure 3, the results suggests that more work is needed to get conclusive results. Consequently, we do not further consider image synthesis here.

3 Experiments

We evaluate the proposed grounding strategies in language modeling and downstream tasks.

3.1 Text-only corpus

Following (Devlin et al., 2019), we use a combination of Wikipedia English pages and the BookCorpus (Zhu et al., 2015) as language modeling corpus. We extract the body of pages from the Wikipedia pages with at least 20 views in the 2013 dump[5], totaling 463k documents, and we sample the same number of passages from the BookCorpus. We call this combination Wiki-BC. We select 90% of the pages/passages as training data, 5% for validation and 5% for test.

3.2 Visuolinguistic corpus

For the **scene-based associations**, we populate the scenes bank M, with the combination of two image captioning datasets. The Stony Brook University corpus (SBU) (Ordonez et al., 2011) is composed of 860k images from the Flickr website, filtered to ensure that the caption literally describes the image. ConceptualCaptions (CC) (Sharma et al., 2018) gathers 3M images that come from web pages that also were heuristically filtered. We use a 90/5/5%

[4] https://deepai.org/machine-learning-model/text2img

[5] Available at https://storage.googleapis.com/lateral-datadumps/wikipedia_utf8_filtered_20pageviews.csv

train/validation/test split for SBU and the standard split for CC.

When performing **object-based associations**, M is populated with ImageNet (Deng et al., 2009). We keep the $15k$ synsets that are associated to at least 10 images, and we randomly sample the images when more are available. Each image is indexed with the average of the lemmas embeddings of its synset, averaged with the embedding of the synset definition.

When performing **transferred grounding**, we concatenate the captioned images (CC-SBU) with our text-only corpus. We sample CC-SBU so that its size matches the text only corpus size (840k passages) to balance the train set. Since our end-goal is text-only processing, we do not use the captioned images in the validation and test set but only in the train set.

In order to test image representations and language modeling on literal text, we also run experiments on the COCO (Lin et al., 2014) dataset made of 400k image/captions pairs. When we do so, we discard the original images when using the associative setup, but we always keep the images in the transferred setup.

3.3 Setup and hyperparameters

We build upon the LXMERT (Tan and Bansal, 2019) code and experimental setup, and rely on its hyperparameters values because of the state-of-the-art results and code availability of this model. Our text encoder is an Albert model pretrained from *albert-base-v2* checkpoint (Lan et al., 2019). Its weights are kept fixed during pretraining and fine-tuned during downstream task training. We use a different copy of this Albert model as the cross-modal encoder initialization and always keep its weights trainable.

In this work, our key/query encoder is a continuous bag of words.We use fastText (Mikolov et al., 2018) embeddings[6] which are competitive with state-of-the-art models on semantic similarity tasks (Reimers and Gurevych, 2019). Queries and keys are matched according to cosine distance with the Faiss (Johnson et al., 2017) library.

Following LXMERT, each image is represented with a sequence N region features. A linear projection maps the region features to the input space of the cross modal encoder. We also provide K rank embeddings which are added to the cross-modal encoder input image representation. Input text is lower-cased and token sequence length is clipped to 64. We use the Adam (Kingma and Ba, 2014) optimizer with a batch size of 32 and a learning rate of 10^{-4} for downstream tasks until convergence on the validation accuracy, with a maximum of 4 epochs. When we retrieve $K = 16$ images [7] with object-based associations, we use $\kappa = 8$ clusters[8]. Following (Tan and Bansal, 2019), we mask 15% of text tokens during the JMLM pretraining; and we use a linear regression head with L_1 regularization for JMRM.

We first compare the expressivity of the image representations in function of their size, then delve into the comparison of grounding strategies, according to JMLM pretraining and downstream tasks scores.

3.4 Efficient image representation

We want to be able to provide $K > 1$ images to the cross-modal encoder. However, the cross-modal encoder memory usage scales quadratically with the number of regions $K.N$, so we will evaluate to what extent $N \gg 1$ is necessary. Previous work use object detection on a single image to find 36 Regions of Interest (RoI) and represents them by ResNet-50 (He et al., 2016) features with 2048 dimensions. We run the JMLM pretraining setup with several image representations. We evaluate two representations: (1) the previously used ResNet region representations provided by (Tan and Bansal, 2019) with various values of N; (2) Single representation of the whole image, using EfficientNet-B1 Noisy Student (Xie et al., 2020) pre-logit max-pooled features. We finetune neither of them.

We use the COCO dataset for this evaluation because its annotations are manual and not heuristically filtered, and because the image features used by (Tan and Bansal, 2019) are publicly available. We evaluate the image representations with JMLM pretraining perplexity. Table 1 shows the results of this experiment. Overall, the presence of image features ($N > 0$) significantly improves the JMLM performance. While the standard FastR-CNN(Girshick, 2015)+ResNet with 16 objects representation achieves the best perplexity (even bet-

[6]We use the CommonCrawl version https://fasttext.cc/docs/en/english-vectors.html. and discard stop-words with NLTK.

[7]We have tested values $\{1, 4, 8, 16, 24\}$ and the lowest Wiki-BC validation perplexity for both object and scene based setups is 16.

[8]We capped this value to 8 since some short texts do not refer to many objects.

N	Features	COCO perplexity
0	-	8.4
1	EfficientNet-1280	4.6
8	ResNet-2048	4.6
16	ResNet-2048	**4.0**
36	ResNet-2048	4.2

Table 1: The effect of image representations on cross-modal JMLM perplexity on the COCO dataset with $K = 1$ image per example; N is the number of visual regions per image.

Strategy	K	Wiki-BC ppl.	COCO ppl.
No Grounding	0	8.7	7.6
Transferred i2t	0/1	30.0	**4.6**
Transferred t2i	0/1	41.6	-
Transferred t2i+i2t	0/1	25.3	-
Associative (Zhang et al., 2020)	16	8.9	8.6
Associative (scene-based)	16	**8.5**	**4.6**
Associative (scene-based)	1	9.1	7.3
Associative (object-based)	1	9.0	35.6
Associative (object-based)	16	8.6	4.7

Table 2: JMLM test perplexity on the Wiki-BC+CC-SBU dataset and on the COCO captions. On the COCO dataset, COCO images are used at test time for the transferred i2t strategy. On the Wiki-BC dataset, the image placeholder is used at test time for the transferred strategies while associative strategies always use associated images.

ter than with 36 features, which can be attributed to a reduced over-fitting), while this performance breaks down with few recognized objects. The performance of EfficientNet representations using the whole image as a single region is competitive while being much lighter. Consequently, in the experiments described in the following section we represent images with EfficientNet-B1 features and $N = 1$ region per image.

4 Empirical comparison of grounding strategies

4.1 JMLM training

We run the pretraining for each strategy on the Wiki-BC corpus, and also run a separate pretraining on the COCO corpus in order to assess language modeling performance on a literal, descriptive domain. Table 2 reports the influence of the grounding strategies on test perplexities. (Zhang et al., 2020) is an image retrieval system ranking the images according to the number of text keywords they contain. It was originally used to improve Neural Machine translation (see Related Work). On the COCO dataset, using the original image paired with the text captions leads to the lowest perplexity, but surprisingly, using $K = 16$ associated object or scenes leads to a competitive perplexity. This suggests than the many distantly related images can be a good substitution to a canonically associated image, even though associating $K = 1$ object seems to be a too noisy signal.

The results on the Wiki-BC dataset reveal a similar pattern. Here, the transferred strategies cannot use images at test time and suffer from a domain shift which leads to inferior results. However, the associative strategies and $K = 16$ lead to the lowest perplexity even though the gap between ungrounded and grounded methods is small than with the COCO dataset due to abstractness of the open-domain texts. We thereby show that even language modeling can benefit from grounding, and the masked language modeling perplexity might translate to yet further applications in text generation (Wang and Cho, 2019). We will now investigate how grounding translates to downstream classification tasks accuracy.

4.2 Downstream evaluation

We hypothesize that grounded models should be better equipped to perform common sense related downstream tasks. A first component of our evaluation on tasks RTE, PDTB and JOCI will test that claim. But we also expect the concreteness to have an influence on the behavior of grounded models. Thus, we also perform a more targeted evaluation on concrete-only examples (SICK) and metaphoricity classification (VUA tasks) to better interpret our results.

Recognizing Textual Entailment (RTE) (Dagan et al., 2006) is a Natural Language Inference (NLI) task. Its dataset gathers sentence pairs with a premise and a hypothesis. The labels describe the logical relationship between the two, that is, entailment and non-entailment.

JHU Ordinal Common-sense Inference (JOCI) (Zhang et al., 2017) The dataset for this task also consists of premise/hypothesis sentence pairs, but the labels are numerical scores from 1 to 5 that reflect the plausibility of the hypothesis given the premise according to human annotators, relying on their own common sense.

Sentences Involving Compositional Knowledge (SICK) (Kiela et al., 2018) is also a NLI dataset with entailment, neutral and contradiction classes

Strategy	Pretraining Text	K	JOCI	PDTB	RTE	SICK	VUA	VUAN	AVG
Albert-base	-	-	6.7	49.6	**68.0**	**88.2**	82.7	85.0	63.4
No-Grounding	Wiki-BK	0	8.7	46.0	56.8	87.4	82.2	83.8	60.8
Transferred i2t	CC-SBU+Wiki-BK	0/1	-0.4	31.1	60.2	85.7	82.1	84.5	57.2
Transferred t2i	CC-SBU+Wiki-BK	0/1	8.3	19.3	65.6	87.4	82.9	84.6	58.0
Transferred t2i+i2t	CC-SBU+Wiki-BK	0/1	**11.1**	**52.0**	61.1	88.0	82.7	**85.2**	63.4
Associative (Zhang et al., 2020)	Wiki-BK	16	2.4	48.4	54.3	87.6	79.6	81.9	59.0
Associative (scene-based)	Wiki-BK	16	1.2	49.3	54.5	86.1	83.0	84.0	59.7
Associative (object-based)	Wiki-BK	16	8.6	50.8	67.6	87.1	**83.1**	84.0	**63.5**

Table 3: Downstream tasks transfer results. Reported score is Spearman's correlation percentage for the JOCI task and accuracy percentage, otherwise. Albert-base is the pretrained model from (Lan et al., 2019) without architectural change or further pretraining before the downstream fine-tuning. Our models are based on Albert-base but have an additional cross-modal transformer that underwent an additional pretraining stage. K is the number of images per example. The No-Grounding setup is equivalent to the transferred setup on Wiki-BK, or the associative setup with $K = 0$.

but it differs from the previous two in that its premises are only composed of image captions and video descriptions. This allows a more specific evaluation of concrete language, as opposed to abstract domain language in the RTE tasks.

Penn Discourse TreeBank (PDTB) (Prasad et al., 2008) contains a collection of fine-grained implicit (i.e., not signaled by a discourse marker) relations between sentences from the news domain in PDTB2.0, which signal the purpose of an utterance given a context utterance. We select level 2 implicit relations as categories. The task involves presupposition recognition and the ability to deal with non-literal meaning.

VU Amsterdam Metaphor Corpus (VUA) (Krennmayr and Steen, 2017) annotates the uses of verbs in sentences of the British National Corpus according to their level of metaphoricity. For instance, in the sentence *The alligator's teeth are like white daggers*, the use of the word *daggers* is metaphorical while *teeth* is not. We use the dataset of a shared task on verb metaphoricity detection (Klebanov et al., 2020) as well as another version where we kept only the nouns which we call VUAN.

Table 4 in appendix A.2 shows the dataset sizes, and Table 3 reports the results of the Wiki-BC trained models on the above tasks. We perform 8 runs for each task and report the median score.

As baselines we propose the Albert-base model alongside an ablated model without visual grounding and a state-of-the-art association model which uses visual input as described by Zhang et al. (2020). The Albert-base model (Lan et al., 2019) is a pretrained transformer that takes the text tokens as inputs and provides a representation of the text examples at the output of the $[CLS]$ token which is used to perform the logistic regression. In the No-Grounding model, the cross-modal encoder is trained on text-only corpus always using the placeholder as visual input. (Zhang et al., 2020) is an image retrieval system that ranks images according to the number of text keywords their captions contain. In this work, the retrieved image features are combined with the source text features to perform neural machine translation. Here, we use this retrieval model with our associative strategy as a baseline.

The No-Grounding model performance does not match the Albert-base model, which indicates that our linguistic pretraining is not as well tuned. However, grounding still yields improvements on the JOCI, PDTB and VUA tasks. The image-to-text (i2t) pretraining does not transfer well in the absence of images. But combining both text-to-image and image-to-text training leads to higher results. This suggests that the resulting model is able to use the obtained multimodal features to better perform the downstream tasks. The performance of the associative strategies depends on the image retrieval system but the comparison suggests that object-based and scene-based retrieval perform well enough to yield meaningful results.

Overall, the object-based associative strategy has the best performance and also performs well on language modeling, especially when generating descriptions. But the transferred strategy seems to be a better choice for the downstream NLP tasks, since it does not require images during fine-tuning and at test time.

5 Related work

Visual grounding has been repeatedly applied in NLP. The specificity of our work lies in the systematic categorization and comparison of grounding strategies, alongside the proposition of image-to-text and associative grounding.

It was shown to improve machine text translation (Specia et al., 2016; Elliott et al., 2017). However, these improvements only affected multimodal translation tasks. Zhang et al. (2020) showed that text-only translation tasks could benefit from external visual knowledge through image search, which we also demonstrate in our associative grounding strategy when applied to different NLP tasks.

Visual grounding has also been applied to transferable word representation learning. Bruni et al. (2014) generalize the distributional hypothesis by extracting discrete visual words from images and using them as context of text while relying on dimensionality reduction. This latter idea is reused with an autoencoder (Silberer and Lapata, 2014) and a SkipGram model (Lazaridou et al., 2015). Kiela and Bottou (2014) combine word embeddings with ImageNet visual features associated to words. Conversely, Collell et al. (2017) learn to predict ImageNet visual features from words and use the predicted *imagined* visual representation as auxiliary features. However, the above techniques are not applicable beyond the word-level. Image captioning datasets do provide sentences associated with relevant images, but the multimodal models trained on these are not commonly used in downstream NLP tasks. Kiela et al. (2018) train sentence embeddings for text processing tasks by learning to predict images from captions and report marginal improvements on SentEval (Conneau and Kiela, 2018) downstream tasks. This approach is similar to our text-to-image transferred grounding. Concurrent work incorporate grounding into Transformers-based pretrained language models (Tan and Bansal, 2020). They match each word in a text-only corpora with an image, and perform a masked image modeling with associated tokens. In our framework, this could be Transferred Associative object-based Grounding.

Other work targets grounded language understanding, but mostly in the context of robotics (Matuszek, 2018) where the text mostly regards task-oriented interactions in a closed-world.

Numerous text-level encoders were recently proposed to leverage images but were only applied to tasks involving both text and images. They all take BERT (Devlin et al., 2019) as a starting point and represent images with region features. They adapt masked language modeling to images with a form of masked image modeling, and each have more specific contributions. For instance, LXMERT (Tan and Bansal, 2019) demonstrates the value of visual question answering as a transferable pretraining task. UNITER (Chen et al., 2020) shows that masked image modeling and masked language modeling are best done separately. VL-BERT (Su et al., 2019) uses an additional text-only training. VilBERT (Lu et al., 2019) proposes a KL-divergence loss for masked image modeling.

Ideas comparable to associative visual grounding have also previously been used with external graph and text data. Liu et al. (2020) leverage triplets found in knowledge bases to better find entities in text. Guu et al. (2020) use language modeling pretraining in order to learn to retrieve and use relevant passages in question answering tasks.

6 Conclusion

In this paper we have proposed visual grounding strategies to make joint text-image models applicable to text-only processing. We have demonstrated that the associative strategy leads to consistent improvements when performing NLP tasks such as masked language modelling, plausibility estimation, metaphoricity detection and discourse relation prediction. Results could be further improved by refining the image representation and retrieval model. Since relying on image captions limited the number of images we could use, it would be interesting to investigate the use of larger-scale image datasets. Further work is needed to refine the effect of multimodality on NLP tasks. It is also interesting to study how NLP performance scales with the sizes of datasets used in pretraining the multimodal representations as is also suggested in (Kaplan et al., 2020).

7 Acknowledgements

This work is part of the CALCULUS5 project, which is funded by the ERC Advanced Grant H2020-ERC-2017 ADG 788506[9].

[9]https://calculus-project.eu/

References

Yonatan Bisk, Ari Holtzman, Jesse Thomason, Jacob Andreas, Yoshua Bengio, Joyce Chai, Mirella Lapata, Angeliki Lazaridou, Jonathan May, Aleksandr Nisnevich, et al. 2020. Experience grounds language. *arXiv preprint arXiv:2004.10151*.

Elia Bruni, Nam-Khanh Tran, and Marco Baroni. 2014. Multimodal distributional semantics. *Journal of Artificial Intelligence Research*, 49:1–47.

Yen-Chun Chen, Linjie Li, Licheng Yu, Ahmed El Kholy, Faisal Ahmed, Zhe Gan, Yu Cheng, and Jingjing Liu. 2020. Uniter: Universal image-text representation learning. In *Proceedings of ECCV*.

Guillem Collell, Ted Zhang, and Marie-Francine Moens. 2017. Imagined visual representations as multimodal embeddings. In *Proceedings of AAAI*.

Alexis Conneau and Douwe Kiela. 2018. SentEval: An evaluation toolkit for universal sentence representations. In *Proceedings of the Eleventh International Conference on Language Resources and Evaluation (LREC 2018)*, Miyazaki, Japan. European Language Resources Association (ELRA).

Ido Dagan, Oren Glickman, and Bernardo Magnini. 2006. The pascal recognising textual entailment challenge. In *Machine Learning Challenges. Evaluating Predictive Uncertainty, Visual Object Classification, and Recognising Tectual Entailment*, pages 177–190, Berlin, Heidelberg. Springer Berlin Heidelberg.

Jia Deng, Wei Dong, Richard Socher, Li-Jia Li, Kai Li, and Li Fei-Fei. 2009. Imagenet: A large-scale hierarchical image database. In *Proceedings of CVPR*, pages 248–255. Ieee.

Jacob Devlin, Ming-Wei Chang, Kenton Lee, and Kristina Toutanova. 2019. BERT: Pre-training of deep bidirectional transformers for language understanding. In *Proceedings of NAACL-HLT Volume 1 (Long and Short Papers)*, pages 4171–4186. ACL.

Desmond Elliott, Stella Frank, Loïc Barrault, Fethi Bougares, and Lucia Specia. 2017. Findings of the second shared task on multimodal machine translation and multilingual image description. In *Proceedings of the Second Conference on Machine Translation*, pages 215–233, Copenhagen, Denmark. Association for Computational Linguistics.

Ross Girshick. 2015. Fast r-cnn. In *Proceedings of ICCV*.

Kelvin Guu, Kenton Lee, Zora Tung, Panupong Pasupat, and Ming-Wei Chang. 2020. Realm: Retrieval-augmented language model pre-training. *arXiv preprint arXiv:2002.08909*.

Kaiming He, Xiangyu Zhang, Shaoqing Ren, and Jian Sun. 2016. Deep residual learning for image recognition. In *Proceedings of CVPR*, pages 770–778.

Jeff Johnson, Matthijs Douze, and Hervé Jégou. 2017. Billion-scale similarity search with gpus. *arXiv preprint arXiv:1702.08734*.

Jared Kaplan, Sam McCandlish, Tom Henighan, Tom B Brown, Benjamin Chess, Rewon Child, Scott Gray, Alec Radford, Jeffrey Wu, and Dario Amodei. 2020. Scaling laws for neural language models. *arXiv preprint arXiv:2001.08361*.

Douwe Kiela and Léon Bottou. 2014. Learning image embeddings using convolutional neural networks for improved multi-modal semantics. In *Proceedings of EMNLP*, pages 36–45. ACL.

Douwe Kiela, Alexis Conneau, Allan Jabri, and Maximilian Nickel. 2018. Learning visually grounded sentence representations. In *Proceedings of NAACL HLT, Volume 1 (Long Papers)*, pages 408–418. ACL.

Douwe Kiela, Felix Hill, Anna Korhonen, and Stephen Clark. 2014. Improving multi-modal representations using image dispersion: Why less is sometimes more. In *Proceedings of ACL (Volume 2: Short Papers)*, pages 835–841. ACL.

Diederik P Kingma and Jimmy Ba. 2014. Adam: A method for stochastic optimization. *arXiv preprint arXiv:1412.6980*.

Beata Beigman Klebanov, Ekaterina Shutova, Patricia Lichtenstein, Smaranda Muresan, Chee Wee, Anna Feldman, and Debanjan Ghosh, editors. 2020. *Proceedings of the Second Workshop on Figurative Language Processing*. ACL.

Tina Krennmayr and Gerard Steen. 2017. Vu amsterdam metaphor corpus. In *Handbook of linguistic annotation*, pages 1053–1071. Springer.

George Lakoff and Mark Johnson. 1980. *Metaphors we Live by*. University of Chicago Press.

Zhenzhong Lan, Mingda Chen, Sebastian Goodman, Kevin Gimpel, Piyush Sharma, and Radu Soricut. 2019. Albert: A lite bert for self-supervised learning of language representations. *arXiv preprint arXiv:1909.11942*.

Angeliki Lazaridou, Nghia The Pham, and Marco Baroni. 2015. Combining language and vision with a multimodal skip-gram model. In *Proceedings of the 2015 Conference of NAACL-HLT*, pages 153–163. ACL.

Tsung-Yi Lin, Michael Maire, Serge Belongie, James Hays, Pietro Perona, Deva Ramanan, Piotr Dollár, and C Lawrence Zitnick. 2014. Microsoft coco: Common objects in context. In *Proceedings of ECCV*, pages 740–755. Springer.

Weijie Liu, Peng Zhou, Zhe Zhao, Zhiruo Wang, Qi Ju, Haotang Deng, and Ping Wang. 2020. K-BERT: Enabling language representation with knowledge graph. In *Proceedings of AAAI 2020*.

Jiasen Lu, Dhruv Batra, Devi Parikh, and Stefan Lee. 2019. Vilbert: Pretraining task-agnostic visiolinguistic representations for vision-and-language tasks. In *Proceedings of NIPS*, pages 13–23.

Cynthia Matuszek. 2018. Grounded language learning: Where robotics and nlp meet. In *Proceedings of IJ-CAI*, pages 5687–5691.

Tomas Mikolov, Edouard Grave, Piotr Bojanowski, Christian Puhrsch, and Armand Joulin. 2018. Advances in pre-training distributed word representations. In *Proceedings of the International Conference on Language Resources and Evaluation (LREC 2018)*.

Timothy Niven and Hung-Yu Kao. 2019. Probing neural network comprehension of natural language arguments. In *Proceedings of ACL*, pages 4658–4664. ACL.

Vicente Ordonez, Girish Kulkarni, and Tamara L. Berg. 2011. Im2text: Describing images using 1 million captioned photographs. In *Proceedings of NIPS*.

Rashmi Prasad, Nikhil Dinesh, Alan Lee, Eleni Miltsakaki, Livio Robaldo, Aravind Joshi, and Bonnie Webber. 2008. The penn discourse treebank 2.0. In *Proceedings of LREC*, Marrakech, Morocco. European Language Resources Association (ELRA).

Nils Reimers and Iryna Gurevych. 2019. Sentence-bert: Sentence embeddings using siamese bert-networks. In *Proceedings of EMNLP*. ACL.

Piyush Sharma, Nan Ding, Sebastian Goodman, and Radu Soricut. 2018. Conceptual captions: A cleaned, hypernymed, image alt-text dataset for automatic image captioning. In *Proceedings of ACL (Volume 1: Long Papers)*, pages 2556–2565. ACL.

Carina Silberer and Mirella Lapata. 2014. Learning grounded meaning representations with autoencoders. In *Proceedings of ACL (Volume 1: Long Papers)*, pages 721–732. ACL.

Lucia Specia, Stella Frank, Khalil Sima'an, and Desmond Elliott. 2016. A shared task on multimodal machine translation and crosslingual image description. In *Proceedings of the First Conference on Machine Translation: Volume 2, Shared Task Papers*, pages 543–553.

Weijie Su, Xizhou Zhu, Yue Cao, Bin Li, Lewei Lu, Furu Wei, and Jifeng Dai. 2019. Vl-bert: Pre-training of generic visual-linguistic representations. *arXiv preprint arXiv:1908.08530*.

Hao Tan and Mohit Bansal. 2019. LXMERT: Learning cross-modality encoder representations from transformers. In *Proceedings of the 2019 Conference on Empirical Methods in Natural Language Processing and the 9th International Joint Conference on Natural Language Processing (EMNLP-IJCNLP)*, pages 5100–5111, Hong Kong, China. Association for Computational Linguistics.

Hao Tan and Mohit Bansal. 2020. Vokenization: Improving language understanding with contextualized, visual-grounded supervision. In *Proceedings of the 2020 Conference on Empirical Methods in Natural Language Processing (EMNLP)*, pages 2066–2080, Online. Association for Computational Linguistics.

Alex Wang and Kyunghyun Cho. 2019. BERT has a mouth, and it must speak: BERT as a Markov random field language model. In *Proceedings of the Workshop on Methods for Optimizing and Evaluating Neural Language Generation*, pages 30–36. ACL.

Alex Wang, Yada Pruksachatkun, Nikita Nangia, Amanpreet Singh, Julian Michael, Felix Hill, Omer Levy, and Samuel R. Bowman. 2019. SuperGLUE: A stickier benchmark for general-purpose language understanding systems. *arXiv preprint 1905.00537*.

Qizhe Xie, Minh-Thang Luong, Eduard Hovy, and Quoc V. Le. 2020. Self-training with noisy student improves imagenet classification. In *Proceedings of the IEEE/CVF Conference on Computer Vision and Pattern Recognition (CVPR)*.

Sheng Zhang, Rachel Rudinger, Kevin Duh, and Benjamin Van Durme. 2017. Ordinal common-sense inference. *Transactions of the Association for Computational Linguistics*, 5:379–395.

Zhuosheng Zhang, Kehai Chen, Rui Wang, Masao Utiyama, Eiichiro Sumita, Zuchao Li, and Hai Zhao. 2020. Neural machine translation with universal visual representation. In *Proceedings of ICLR*.

Yukun Zhu, Ryan Kiros, Rich Zemel, Ruslan Salakhutdinov, Raquel Urtasun, Antonio Torralba, and Sanja Fidler. 2015. Aligning books and movies: Towards story-like visual explanations by watching movies and reading books. In *Proceedings of ICCV*.

A Appendix

A.1 Image association systems

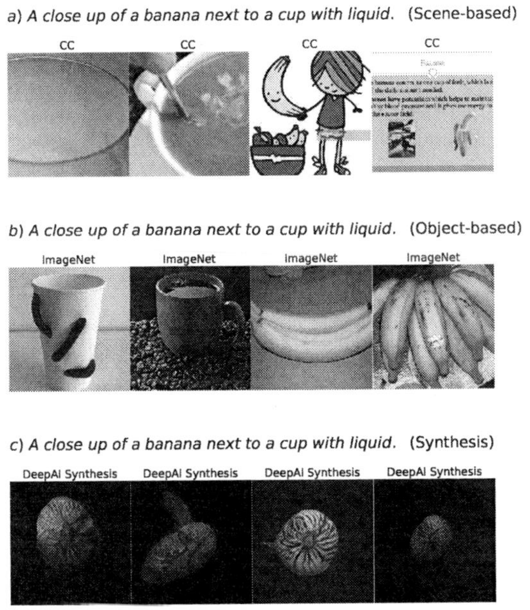

Figure 4: Association of images with a random text sample from the COCO dataset, with scene-based and object-based matching with $K = 4$ and $\kappa = 2$. Scene-based matching (a) indexes images by their caption embedding to match it with the input text. CC refers to the Conceptual Captions dataset. Object-based matching (b) identifies key concepts and matches them with ImageNet images. The Synthesis (c) example illustrates the failure of the DeepAI image synthesis system when the input text is out of domain.

A.2 Downstream tasks sizes

Task	#Examples (Train/Val/Test)	#Labels
JOCI	2.4k/299/298	-
RTE	2.2k/249/277	2
SICK	4.5k/500/4.9k	3
PDTB	12.9k/1.2k/1.1k	16
VUAN	5.0k/1.3k/2.2k	2
VUA	16k/1.7k/5.9k	2

Table 4: Dataset sizes for each downstream task

Exploiting Image-Text Synergy for Contextual Image Captioning

Sreyasi Nag Chowdhury* sreyasi@mpi-inf.mpg.de
Rajarshi Bhowmik† rajarshi.bhowmik@rutgers.edu
Hareesh Ravi† hr268@rutgers.edu
Gerard de Melo†‡ gdm@demelo.org
Simon Razniewski* srazniew@mpi-inf.mpg.de
Gerhard Weikum* weikum@mpi-inf.mpg.de

*Max Planck Institute for Informatics † Rutgers University ‡ Hasso Plattner Institute

Abstract

Modern web content – news articles, blog posts, educational resources, marketing brochures – is predominantly multimodal. A notable trait is the inclusion of media such as images placed at meaningful locations within a textual narrative. Most often, such images are accompanied by captions – either factual or stylistic (humorous, metaphorical, etc.) – making the narrative more engaging to the reader. While standalone image captioning has been extensively studied, captioning an image based on external knowledge such as its surrounding text remains under-explored. In this paper, we study this new task: given an image and an associated unstructured knowledge snippet, the goal is to generate a *contextual caption* for the image.

I recently moved to Buffalo, NY and every day I am discovering how beautiful this town is. I took this pic...and I was thrilled about it! I wanted to share the pallet of colors the sunset had that evening.

Generated Contextual Captions:
- *A beautiful sunset path to heaven.*
- *A sunset...unknown artist.*

Figure 1: Our novel *Contextual Captions* capture the affective theme from a given image and its associated paragraph.

1 Introduction

In multimodal (image–text) documents, images are typically accompanied by captions. These may contain specific knowledge about the narrative – location, names of persons etc. – or may exhibit thematic knowledge grounding the sentimental value of the image in the narrative. The image captions explicitly or implicitly refer to the image and its surrounding text, and play a major role in engaging the reader. We call this type of captions *contextual captions*, and Figure 1 illustrates the corresponding *Contextual Image Captioning* problem.

Generating captions for standalone images (Hossain et al., 2019; Wang et al., 2020) or summarizing a piece of text (See et al., 2017; Lin and Ng, 2019) are well-studied problems. However, generating image captions accounting for contextual knowledge is a largely unexplored task and poses many challenges. Related tasks include multimodal summarization (Chen and Zhuge, 2018, 2019a) and title generation (Murao et al., 2019). Multimodal summarization usually involves segmentation and sorting of both the modalities or has specific templates along which the summary is generated (See et al., 2017). In contrast, generating contextual captions requires conditionally deciding to follow, lead or negate the knowledge offered by the context.

Inadequacy of Prior Work. Image captioning and text summarization are unimodal, and ignore information present in the dormant modality. Multimodal summarization and news image captioning (Biten et al., 2019) usually entail captions with explicit references to the context, and may be achieved with a copy mechanism (Gu et al., 2016) that can selectively copy information (e.g., named entities such as names of people, organizations, geographical locations etc.) from the surrounding text to the caption. However, most social media driven content is affective and requires implicit reasoning about the context. For example, for an image of the Grand Canyon, we might encounter captions such as "perfect for a lovely hike" or "too tired to walk", due to the subjectivity of the task, which requires inference based on the context.

Proceedings of the Third Workshop on Beyond Vision and LANguage: inTEgrating Real-world kNowledge (LANTERN), pages 30–37
Kyiv, Ukraine (Online), April 20, 2021

Approach and Contribution.

- We formulate the novel task of *Contextual Image Captioning* and create a new dataset from Reddit posts with images, titles and comments.
- We propose an end-to-end trained neural model for the *Contextual Image Captioning* task and comprehensively evaluate its performance using quantitative and qualitative measures.
- We study how various factors affect the generation of novel *contextual captions*.

To foster follow-up research we release the dataset and code, available at `https://github.com/Sreyasi/contextual_captions`.

2 Related Work

Image Captioning. Prior work on captioning conditioned only on images (Farhadi et al., 2010; Vinyals et al., 2015; Karpathy and Li, 2015; Krause et al., 2017) has been successful for descriptive captions with explicit grounding to image objects. Recently, captions with sentimental and abstract concepts have been explored (Gan et al., 2017; Chandrasekaran et al., 2018; Park et al., 2017; Liu et al., 2018; Shuster et al., 2019). Although external knowledge bases like DBpedia (factual knowledge) (Wu et al., 2018) and ConceptNet (commonsense knowledge) (Zhou et al., 2019) have been leveraged, all prior work ignores the knowledge present in the text surrounding images in social media and other domains. *Contextual Image Captioning* leverages the latter kind of knowledge.

Multimodal Summarization. Research on multimodal embeddings (Laina et al., 2019; Xia et al., 2020; Scialom et al., 2020) has facilitated studying image–text data. Summarization of multimodal documents (Chu and Kao, 2017; Zhu et al., 2018; Hessel et al., 2019) proceeds by aligning a subset of images with extracted (Chen and Zhuge, 2019a), or generated (Chen and Zhuge, 2018) text segments from the original document. In contrast, image captions in our dataset do not explicitly summarize the associated text and rather act as a short commentary that captures knowledge from both modalities.

News Image Captioning. A task similar to our problem is captioning images within news articles (Tran et al., 2020; Chen and Zhuge, 2019b). A key challenge here is to correctly identify and generate named entities (Tran et al., 2020). However, news image captions tend to be descriptive compared to the subjective nature of captions in our dataset representing common social media content.

3 Datasets

To the best of our knowledge, the only existing image–text caption datasets are from the news domain (e.g., Daily Mail Corpus) containing non-affective descriptive captions with mentions of named entities. Instead, we consider Reddit, which offers a rich source of multimodal data. Out of the image-related subreddits, /r/pics is particularly suitable for our problem because of the nature of posts. Firstly, the posts do not contain expert jargon, unlike other subreddits like /r/photographs. Secondly, the image captions are mostly affective and not drab descriptions. Lastly, post frequency is high, presenting a big dataset.

Data Scraping. We scrape the subreddit /r/pics to collect 250,000 posts over the span of a year. For each post, we grab the image, the post title, and 1-10 comments. We consider the post title as ground truth caption since it is written by the image poster, ensuring a consistent and coherent intent. The comments are concatenated, preserving their tree structure, to serve as the unstructured knowledge associated with the image. Inappropriate posts that do not adhere to community standards and were flagged by moderators are removed.

Data Characteristics. The collected images do not adhere to any particular subject or theme. The paragraphs are ~59.2 words long, and the captions are ~10.6 words long on an average.

In some posts, captions and comments may contain different named entities (NE), making prediction of the ground truth NE difficult. For example, the caption "My friend and I are en route to the Grand Canyon" may be accompanied with the comment "Try to hike down to the Colorado. Also visit Zion National Park!" The NEs in the paragraph (Colorado, Zion) do not match that in the caption (Grand Canyon). Owing to this characteristic, we study two distinct variants of the dataset – one containing NEs and the other without NEs. We denote these variants as *+NE* and ~~*NE*~~, respectively.

The comments sometimes exhibit topic drift, e.g., a comment on the Grand Canyon post may be "I remember my last trip to India...we had spicy food!". Hence, we also study variants with ensured context overlap – one common word (ignoring stop words) between caption and comments. These variants are suffixed *overlap* – e.g. *+NE-overlap*.

We report experimental results on all of these variants, adopting a 30,000/8,000/8,000 train/val/test split for each of them.

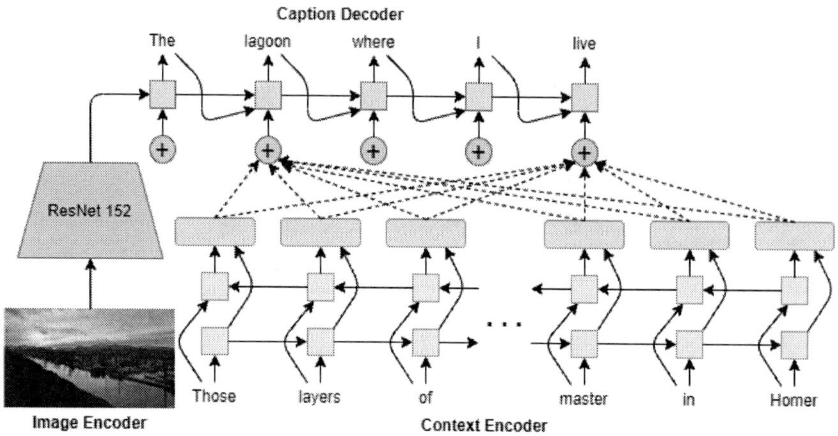

Figure 2: A schematic diagram of our contextual captioning model

4 Contextual Captioning Model

We refer to the text context associated with each image as 'paragraph'. This offers external knowledge which may be absent in the image modality alone. Figure 2 shows our proposed model architecture. Given an input image I and an associated input paragraph $P = \{w_1^p, \ldots, w_M^p\}$ of length M, our model (an encoder–decoder architecture) generates a caption $C = \{w_1^c, \ldots, w_N^c\}$ of length N. For image encoding, we use features extracted from a pre-trained ResNet152 (He et al., 2016) model.

To encode the input paragraph, we deploy a bidirectional LSTM (BiLSTM). The outputs of the BiLSTM, denoted as $\mathbf{G} = \{\mathbf{g}_1, \ldots, \mathbf{g}_M\}$, where $\mathbf{g}_i = \text{BiLSTM}(\mathbf{x}_i, \mathbf{g}_{i-1}) \forall i \in i \in \{1, \ldots, M\}$, is the encoded representation of the input paragraph. $\mathbf{x}_i$ is the vector embedding of the word w_i^p.

We deploy a unidirectional LSTM for sequential decoding of the caption C that leverages both the encoded image and paragraph representations. The image embedding is provided as an input to the decoder LSTM at timestep $t = 1$. In all subsequent timesteps, the decoder input is the embedding $\mathbf{y}_{t-1}$ of the previous token w_{t-1}^c. The decoder state at each timestep t is obtained as $\mathbf{h}_t = \text{LSTM}(\mathbf{y}_{t-1}, \mathbf{h}_{t-1})$. To incorporate contextual information from the input paragraph, we concatenate an attention-weighted sum of the encoder states, denoted as $\tilde{\mathbf{G}}_t$, to the current state $\mathbf{h}_t$.

At each decoder time step $t \in \{2, \ldots N\}$, the attention weights α^t over the encoder states depend on the current decoder state $\mathbf{h_t}$ and the encoder states $\mathbf{G}$. Formally,

$$\tilde{\mathbf{G}}_\mathbf{t} = \sum_{i=i}^{M} \alpha_i^t \mathbf{g_i} \tag{1}$$

$$\alpha_i^t = \frac{\mathbf{v}^\intercal(\mathbf{W_g g_i} + \mathbf{W_h h_t} + \mathbf{b})}{\sum_{i'=1}^{M} \mathbf{v}^\intercal(\mathbf{W_g g_{i'}} + \mathbf{W_h h_t} + \mathbf{b})} \tag{2}$$

Finally, we pass the concatenated output through two dense layers with a non-linear activation layer (e.g, ReLU) placed in between. The output logits are then passed through a Softmax function to obtain the output distribution $p(.)$ over the vocabulary. We train our model end-to-end by minimizing the negative log-likelihood, i.e., $\theta^* = \text{argmin}_\theta - \log p(C \mid I, P; \theta)$. Note that we obtain the input embeddings, $\mathbf{x_i}$, and $\mathbf{y_t}$, of the encoder and decoder, respectively, from the embedding layer of a pretrained $\text{BERT}_{\text{BASE}}$ model.

The model's objective is to learn the optimal parameters θ^* to maximize the log-likelihood $\log p(C|I, P; \theta)$. Therefore, we train our model end-to-end by minimizing the negative log-likelihood defined as:

$$\mathcal{L}(\theta) = \sum_{t=1}^{N} - \log p(w_t^c \mid w_1^c, \ldots, w_{t-1}^c, I, P; \theta) \tag{3}$$

5 Experiments and Results

5.1 Quantitative Evaluation

Metrics. We use the MSCOCO (Lin et al., 2014) automatic caption evaluation tool[1] to quantitatively evaluate our proposed model variants using the BLEU-1, ROUGE-L, CIDEr, and SPICE

[1]https://github.com/tylin/coco-caption

	BLEU-1	*ROUGE-L*	*CIDEr*	*SPICE*	*SemSim*
		+NE			
Image-only	**9.72**	**8.42**	0.42	0.18	**0.72**
Text-only	8.71	7.85	**0.68**	**0.29**	0.73
Contextual	7.94	7.82	0.50	0.17	0.71
		+NE-overlap			
Image-only	8.64	7.84	0.50	0.19	0.73
Text-only	8.34	7.48	0.53	0.20	0.73
Contextual	**10.13**	**9.57**	**0.84**	**0.31**	**0.75**
		~~NE~~			
Image-only	5.96	6.42	0.37	0.14	0.71
Text-only	5.36	5.29	0.30	0.16	0.68
Contextual	**6.37**	**6.93**	**0.45**	**0.19**	**0.72**
		~~NE~~-overlap			
Image-only	7.80	7.50	0.38	0.16	0.76
Text-only	6.87	6.54	0.61	0.36	0.72
Contextual	**9.30**	**9.68**	**0.78**	**0.50**	**0.77**

Table 1: Quantitative Evaluation of baselines and Contextual Captioning on different data splits

Image		
Paragraph	Made the hike to Franklin Falls and while waiting for some other people to clear my shot, I noticed how good the light looked hitting the rocks.	I was driving down the mountain... popped out my camera to snag this shot. It's beautiful right now... there wasn't nearly as much snow as last year.
Contextual	*Rush hour on the nature coast.*	*I love the snow mountains. Come in the countryside often.*
Image-only	*The view from the top of the cosmopolitan.*	*The view from the top of the moon.*
Text-only	*Pretty cool sunset.*	*Rain ready for a local bar.*

Figure 3: Linguistic richness of *Contextual Captions* in contrast to those generated from only image or only text.

metrics. In addition, we also report scores for semantic similarity between ground truth (c_{gt}) and generated (c_{gen}) captions: $\text{SemSim}(c_{\text{gt}}, c_{\text{gen}}) = \text{cosine}(\mathbf{v}_{c_{\text{gt}}}, \mathbf{v}_{c_{\text{gen}}})$, where $\mathbf{v}_{c_{\text{gt}}}$ and $\mathbf{v}_{c_{\text{gen}}}$ are the mean vectors of constituent words in the respective captions from 300-dimensional GloVe embeddings.

Baselines. To the best of our knowledge, there is no existing work that studies contextual image captioning. Therefore, we present two baselines that can also be regarded as ablated versions of our model: *Image-only* and *Text-only* captioning.

Results. In Table 1, we report scores[2] for the baselines and our model variants. Recall from Section 3 that our models are based on various data splits: *+NE*, *~~NE~~*, and their respective *overlap* variants. We observe that for the *+NE* split, contextual captions are not better than the unimodal baselines on n-gram overlap based scores. This can be attributed to the nature of the dataset: NEs in the paragraph differ from those in ground truth captions. Since contextual captions draw inference from the paragraphs, the predicted NEs differ from ground truth captions as well, leading to lower scores for n-gram overlap based metrics. For the ~~NE~~ splits as well as both the *overlap* splits, contextual captions fare better than the baselines.

The observed low scores for BLEU-1, ROUGE-L, CIDEr and SPICE hint towards the subjectivity of the task. N-gram overlap based metrics do not accommodate varied interpretations and linguistic diversity. Figure 3 exemplifies how image-only captions for different images are often similar, while contextual captions are linguistically richer.

High average SemSim scores of contextual captions are indicative of their thematic similarity with the ground truth. Note that the splits with enforced similarity (*-overlap*) between paragraph and caption fare better on SemSim, leading to the conjecture that with a cleaner dataset, it would be possible to generate very relevant contextual captions.

5.2 Qualitative Evaluation

Setup. The scope of this evaluation is to analyze the different splits of our dataset. A user study was set up on the crowd-sourcing platform Appen[3]. 250 test samples were studied. For each sample, users were shown the image and its associated paragraph, and were asked to rate 6 captions (4 contextual captions and 2 baselines from Table 1) on a scale from 1 (irrelevant) to 5 (highly relevant).

Observations. We observe that for 80% of samples (201 out of 250), at least one of the 4 contextual captioning models is rated strictly higher than both baselines, and for 95% of samples they are at least as good as both baselines. A variant-wise analysis of this is shown in Table 2.

In 75% of samples, contextual captions were rated highest among all 6 captions. The variant-wise analysis of the same is shown in Table 3.

We identify three categories of samples:

[2]The BLEU-1 and ROUGE-L scores are multiplied by 100, and CIDEr and SPICE scores are multiplied by 10 following the standard practice.

[3]`https://appen.com`, formerly named *Figure8*.

Table 2: Percentage of samples where contextual captions are rated as good as or better than baselines.

	Image-only		Text-only	
	≥	>	≥	>
+NE	71.6	42.4	74.4	38.4
+NE-overlap	69.6	42.8	74.0	44.4
~~NE~~	70.0	45.2	73.6	41.2
~~NE~~-overlap	**76.0**	**48.4**	**81.2**	**49.6**

Table 3: Percentage of samples rated highest per model.

+NE	+NE-overlap	~~NE~~	~~NE~~-overlap	Image-only	Text-only
17.8	15.8	15.9	**25.7**	15.0	9.9

- *Significant*: samples where at least one of the 6 variants generate a caption with rating ≥ 3. These constitute 46% of samples (115/250).
- *Insignificant*: samples on which all 6 variants obtain a rating < 3. Here, paragraphs show substantial randomness and offer little context for the image. It appears impossible to generate good contextual captions for such samples.
- *Bad-base*: samples which are insignificant (rating < 3) with respect to both baselines. These constitute 80% of samples (201/250).

For 86% of *Significant* samples (99/115), contextual captions were rated higher than the baselines. A detailed analysis is given in Table 4.

Table 4: Percentage of *Significant* samples where contextual captions are rated as good as or better than baselines.

	Image-only		Text-only	
	≥	>	≥	>
+NE	66.1	55.7	67.8	47.0
+NE-overlap	64.4	53.9	69.6	54.0
~~NE~~	60.9	48.7	64.4	43.5
~~NE~~-overlap	**72.2**	**59.1**	**78.3**	**58.3**

The ratings of 33% (67 of 201) of *Bad-base* samples were made significant, i.e., improved to strictly ≥ 3, by the best contextual captioning model variant. In other words, contextual captioning generates superior captions for samples with inferior baseline captions.

~~NE~~-overlap emerged as the best-suited contextual captioning variant in both quantitative and qualitative evaluations.

Factorial Experiment. We conduct another study taking the form of a $2 \times 2 \times 2$ full factorial experiment based on three factors – presence of NEs, caption-paragraph overlap, and use of pre-trained BERT token embeddings. We study the effect of these factors with a user study with all factor combinations. The effect of each of the factors can be seen in Figure 4. Using BERT token embeddings is by far the most effective in enhancing caption quality. It is interesting to note that presence of NEs (including its interaction with other factors) has a negative effect – captions without NEs are rated higher by human evaluators. Caption-paragraph overlap splits are also rated higher, which indicates that high inter-modality content overlap is necessary for generating good contextual captions.

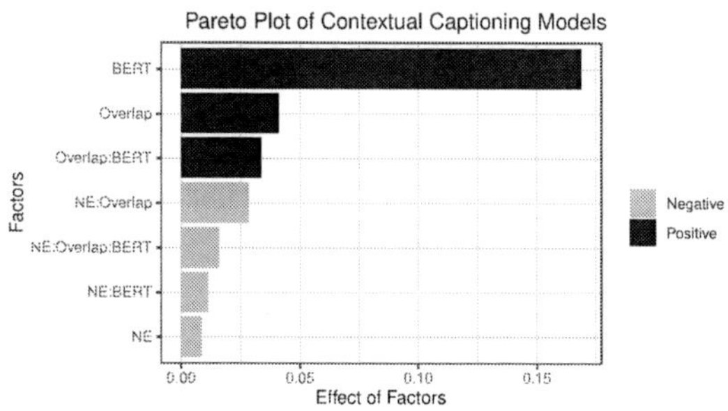

Figure 4: Effect of various factors in Contextual Captioning.

5.3 Discussion

Named Entities in Captions. Our user study shows that contextual captions with named entities (NE) are less preferred by humans. We conjecture that a lack of strong cues from the paragraphs lead to incorrectly generated NEs. Future work should also explore copy mechanisms to copy NEs from paragraphs to captions.

Caption Quality. We observe that the baseline captions do not show linguistic diversity (Figure 3). "The view from...", "My friend and I..." etc. are common templates learned by the models. We conjecture that training the model on samples containing coherent paragraphs that have high content overlap with the image would yield nicer captions. We partially emulate this in our *-overlap* splits, which indeed show better model performance.

6 Conclusion

We propose the novel task of *Contextual Image Captioning* that exploits complementary knowledge from different modalities in multimodal contents. To facilitate a thorough study of this task, we curate a new dataset comprising ~250,000 multimodal Reddit posts. We provide an analysis of the dataset along with experimental results to identify interesting factors that determine the quality of generated contextual captions. We hope that our work will kindle and support follow-up research on this under-explored task, with downstream applications such as content authoring tools and multimodal conversational agents.

References

Ali Furkan Biten, Lluís Gómez, Marçal Rusiñol, and Dimosthenis Karatzas. 2019. acute; good news, everyone! context driven entity-aware captioning for news images. In *CVPR*.

Arjun Chandrasekaran, Devi Parikh, and Mohit Bansal. 2018. Punny captions: Witty wordplay in image descriptions. In *NAACL-HLT*.

Jingqiang Chen and Hai Zhuge. 2018. Abstractive text-image summarization using multi-modal attentional hierarchical RNN. In *EMNLP*.

Jingqiang Chen and Hai Zhuge. 2019a. Extractive summarization of documents with images based on multi-modal RNN. *Future Gener. Comput. Syst.*

Jingqiang Chen and Hai Zhuge. 2019b. News image captioning based on text summarization using image as query. In *SKG*.

Wei-Ta Chu and Ming-Chih Kao. 2017. Blog article summarization with image-text alignment techniques. In *ISM*.

Ali Farhadi, Seyyed Mohammad Mohsen Hejrati, Mohammad Amin Sadeghi, Peter Young, Cyrus Rashtchian, Julia Hockenmaier, and David A. Forsyth. 2010. Every picture tells a story: Generating sentences from images. In *ECCV*.

Chuang Gan, Zhe Gan, Xiaodong He, Jianfeng Gao, and Li Deng. 2017. Stylenet: Generating attractive visual captions with styles. In *CVPR*.

Jiatao Gu, Zhengdong Lu, Hang Li, and Victor O. K. Li. 2016. Incorporating copying mechanism in sequence-to-sequence learning. In *ACL*.

K. He, X. Zhang, S. Ren, and J. Sun. 2016. Deep residual learning for image recognition. In *CVPR*.

Jack Hessel, Lillian Lee, and David Mimno. 2019. Unsupervised discovery of multimodal links in multi-image, multi-sentence documents. In *EMNLP/IJCNLP*.

MD Hossain, Ferdous Sohel, Mohd Fairuz Shiratuddin, and Hamid Laga. 2019. A comprehensive survey of deep learning for image captioning. *ACM Computing Surveys (CSUR)*, 51(6):118.

Andrej Karpathy and Fei-Fei Li. 2015. Deep visual-semantic alignments for generating image descriptions. In *CVPR*.

Jonathan Krause, Justin Johnson, Ranjay Krishna, and Li Fei-Fei. 2017. A hierarchical approach for generating descriptive image paragraphs. In *CVPR*.

Iro Laina, Christian Rupprecht, and Nassir Navab. 2019. Towards unsupervised image captioning with shared multimodal embeddings. In *ICCV*.

Hui Lin and Vincent Ng. 2019. Abstractive summarization: A survey of the state of the art. In *AAAI*.

Tsung-Yi Lin, Michael Maire, Serge J. Belongie, James Hays, Pietro Perona, Deva Ramanan, Piotr Dollár, and C. Lawrence Zitnick. 2014. Microsoft COCO: common objects in context. In *ECCV*.

Bei Liu, Jianlong Fu, Makoto P. Kato, and Masatoshi Yoshikawa. 2018. Beyond narrative description: Generating poetry from images by multi-adversarial training. In *ACM Multimedia*.

Kazuma Murao, Ken Kobayashi, Hayato Kobayashi, Taichi Yatsuka, Takeshi Masuyama, Tatsuru Higurashi, and Yoshimune Tabuchi. 2019. A case study on neural headline generation for editing support. In *NAACL-HLT*.

Cesc Chunseong Park, Byeongchang Kim, and Gunhee Kim. 2017. Attend to you: Personalized image captioning with context sequence memory networks. In *CVPR*.

Thomas Scialom, Patrick Bordes, Paul-Alexis Dray, Jacopo Staiano, and Patrick Gallinari. 2020. BERT can see out of the box: On the cross-modal transferability of text representations. *CoRR*.

Abigail See, Peter J. Liu, and Christopher D. Manning. 2017. Get to the point: Summarization with pointer-generator networks. In *ACL*.

Kurt Shuster, Samuel Humeau, Hexiang Hu, Antoine Bordes, and Jason Weston. 2019. Engaging image captioning via personality. In *CVPR*.

Alasdair Tran, Alexander Mathews, and Lexing Xie. 2020. Transform and Tell: Entity-Aware News Image Captioning. In *CVPR*.

Oriol Vinyals, Alexander Toshev, Samy Bengio, and Dumitru Erhan. 2015. Show and tell: A neural image caption generator. In *CVPR*.

Haoran Wang, Yue Zhang, and Xiaosheng Yu. 2020. An overview of image caption generation methods. *Comp. Int. and Neurosc.*, 2020:3062706:1–3062706:13.

Qi Wu, Chunhua Shen, Peng Wang, Anthony R. Dick, and Anton van den Hengel. 2018. Image captioning and visual question answering based on attributes and external knowledge. *IEEE Trans. Pattern Anal. Mach. Intell.*

Qiaolin Xia, Haoyang Huang, Nan Duan, Dongdong Zhang, Lei Ji, Zhifang Sui, Edward Cui, Taroon Bharti, Xin Liu, and Ming Zhou. 2020. XGPT: cross-modal generative pre-training for image captioning. *CoRR*.

Yimin Zhou, Yiwei Sun, and Vasant G. Honavar. 2019. Improving image captioning by leveraging knowledge graphs. In *WACV*.

Junnan Zhu, Haoran Li, Tianshang Liu, Yu Zhou, Jiajun Zhang, and Chengqing Zong. 2018. MSMO: multimodal summarization with multimodal output. In *EMNLP*.

A Appendix

A.1 Dataset Details

- Total number of samples: 242,767
- Samples with named entities (NE) in caption: 137,732 (56.82%)
- Samples with no NE in caption: 104,653 (43.18%)

We ensure a context overlap between paragraph and caption with the following splits:

- *+NE* samples with one common word between paragraph and caption: 50,730 (20.93%). These are named *+NE-overlap* in Table 1.
- *+NE* samples with two common words between paragraph and caption: 23,283 (9.61%).
- *~~NE~~* samples with one common word between paragraph and caption: 38,301 (15.80%). These are named *~~NE~~-overlap* in Table 1.
- *~~NE~~* samples with two common words between paragraph and caption: 15,070 (6.22%)

We use SpaCy to detect named entities in captions. SpaCy detects 18 kinds of named entities[4]. `TIME`, `MONEY`, `PERCENT`, and `LANGUAGE` were not considered since they include common conversational phrases like "day before yesterday", "my two cents", "an English breakfast" etc. Examples of captions with NEs: "Just the (Earth/LOC) letting off some steam (Iceland/GPE)", "The (first/CARDINAL) Chipotle , opened in (Denver/GPE) in (1993/DATE)." Examples of captions without NEs: "Texture of the paint on a skull I painted.", "My girlfriend and I handle social situations differently."

In future work, the NE types could be leveraged to learn positional relationships in sentences.

A.2 Experimental Setup

Our architecture is developed in PyTorch. The number of samples in all train/val/test splits is 30,000/8000/8000. Each model is trained for 20 epochs, with a batch size of 16. On a Tesla V100-PCIE-16 GB GPU, training 1 epoch taken 8 min.

For each model variant, the best validation model is used for testing. We experiment with models using pre-trained BERT token embeddings, as well as learning token embeddings from scratch (with a vocabulary size of 100,000). We observe that BERT token embeddings have a positive effect on the quality of captions (Figure 4), and hence consider this configuration as default.

A.3 Quantitative Evaluation

Validation Performances of Test Models. We train each model for 20 epochs and chose the best validation model for testing. In Table 5 we report the validation losses of our reported test models.

Table 5: Validation loss of the reported test models.

Models	+NE	+NE-overlap	~~NE~~	~~NE~~-overlap
Image-only	0.89	0.70	1.41	1.05
Text-only	1.39	1.46	1.38	1.27
Contextual	1.29	1.28	1.14	1.13

A.4 Examples

Table 5 shows a few good and bad examples of contextual captions.

[4] `https://spacy.io/api/annotation#named-entities`

Image				
Paragraph	Shes pretty. Sorry for your loss. If only dogs had a longer lifespan than humans! If only we picked the one that would bury us. ...That aside, I see you made each others life wonderful.	Thats a dope shot, nice. Thats cool Looks like the Rouge River. Arent those tunnels better known as bridges ? Its not really a bridge its not used for people to get across.	Lenticular clouds are cool... Super cool! Looks like a giant tree... These are called lenticular clouds. This must be the most enticing pic of a mountain I ever saw.	I hope it has LED lights too for full 90s effect... Happy new year bro! That view is majestic. Doesn't look like that thing even plays CDs. You're right.
Contextual Captions	*My only friend passed away last year. He passed away from cancer.*	*A beautiful stream I encountered on holiday.*	*Some of these clouds are having fun as we get out of water.*	*I took this picture of my friends living room in the mountains where the view is breathtaking.*
Image-only Captions	*My friend is a new friend. My son's dog.*	*A picture I took at a morning in my hometown.*	*A picture I took in my morning. The view from my hotel.*	*A picture i took in my local park.*
Text-Only Captions	*Rest easy, hear surgery. Cancer, and essa. He died last year.*	*Milky way over the clouds worth it however.*	*A collage from the top of a cliff bench at midnight.*	*Usually a replica of the most beautiful cities in the world before going to Inverness, France*

Image	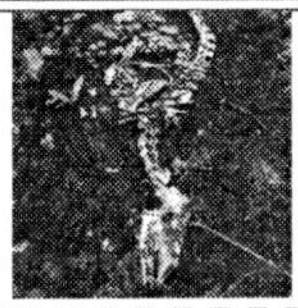			
Paragraph	You absolute legend you. Thanks so much! I saw it and thought the same thing! I tried r/skeletons just gave me spooky bone memes. I'll check fossils though! One of those students are headed to krypton.	there is nothing NSFW about this Beijing agent says what...US says HK police can handle this...HK ppl says please stop violence...I say i am just a HK citizen...Cop used to be an adventurer.	The Jefferson Memorial will always be my favorite DC monument. I've lived in the area for fifteen years and *finally* saw this beauty for myself in person. It was absolutely worth the hellish traffic!	Bird on a Wire. I saw it once on a Leonard Cohen album... Definitely a starling. The Counting Crow Power Line Black Bird. Put a bird on it Definitely a European Starling, it's the most common bird in the world.
Contextual Captions	*I drew this and I thought It looked cool. I want to be a good artist.*	*This is a real unedited picture ever taken.*	*A beautiful sunset ship swallowed sea lion waterfalls.*	*This bird looks like a warrior bird dead bird bird, bird bird dead*
Image-only Captions	*My first time on a year ago, and I just got a photo of this photo.*	*My first ever attempt at a photo of a year ago.*	*The view from my house in the morning.*	*My friend drew this in 1995 today, the delicious*
Text-Only Captions	*Danny Devito ink drawing lights up optical.*	*Hong Kong protesters fired a letter to the protest police threatening by police. Pepper spray*	*Tragedy in Pittsburgh, pa 18 years final night the highway.*	*Hummingbird from the moon landing. I think this is beautiful.*

Figure 5: Good examples (top row) and bad examples (bottom row) of *Contextual Captions*.

Large-Scale Zero-Shot Image Classification from Rich and Diverse Textual Descriptions

Sebastian Bujwid
KTH Royal Institute of Technology
Stockholm, Sweden
`bujwid@kth.se`

Josephine Sullivan
KTH Royal Institute of Technology
Stockholm, Sweden
`sullivan@kth.se`

Abstract

We study the impact of using rich and diverse textual descriptions of classes for zero-shot learning (ZSL) on ImageNet. We create a new dataset *ImageNet-Wiki* that matches each ImageNet class to its corresponding Wikipedia article. We show that merely employing these Wikipedia articles as class descriptions yields much higher ZSL performance than prior works. Even a simple model using this type of auxiliary data outperforms state-of-the-art models that rely on standard features of word embedding encodings of class names. These results highlight the usefulness and importance of textual descriptions for ZSL, as well as the relative importance of auxiliary data type compared to algorithmic progress. Our experimental results also show that standard zero-shot learning approaches generalize poorly across categories of classes.

1 Introduction

Zero-shot learning (ZSL) relates information from different modalities (e.g., text or attributes with images), and the hope is that a sparsity of information or training data in one modality can be compensated by the other. This is important when the cost of creation or collection of training data greatly differs between the different modalities. Natural language descriptions and existing text repositories can provide this rich and practically accessible information about visual concepts and classes when no accompanying labeled images are available.

Recent works on zero-shot image classification (Xian et al., 2019; Schonfeld et al., 2019; Xian et al., 2018) show the field's substantial progress on many of the standard ZSL benchmarks. However, most of those benchmarks mostly cover either a very small or narrow set of classes (e.g., only bird species), where human-made class attributes are often used as auxiliary data. Unfortunately, on ImageNet, where such attributes are not available, the performance is still very low. Therefore, in this work, rather than focus on algorithmic development, we instead study how the auxiliary data type impacts performance. We evaluate the benefits of using textual descriptions of the ImageNet classes. We collect text from Wikipedia articles describing each class in ImageNet, illustrated in Figure 1. Throughout the paper, we refer to the dataset of ImageNet classes and their corresponding Wikipedia articles, as well as the extracted text, as *ImageNet-Wiki*.[1]

The use of textual descriptions for ZSL has been studied before on smaller datasets (Reed et al., 2016; Elhoseiny et al., 2016, 2017; Zhu et al., 2018). However, this is the first work to use such textual descriptions on a large dataset, with a broad set of classes. The major differences between commonly used datasets are highlighted in Table 1. The large-scale setup enables us to study the main challenges of a more realistic and practical zero-shot image classification scenario and study the generalization of models to novel groups of classes (e.g., animal species in general), not only individual classes (e.g., specific animal species).

Our experimental results lead us to two significant observations. First, models using the textual descriptions perform much better than those using class name features. Remarkably, a simple ZSL model based on DeViSE (Frome et al., 2013) and trained on text from *ImageNet-Wiki* clearly outperforms more recent, state-of-the-art models that use word embedding features of class names as the auxiliary data. For the CADA-VAE model (Schonfeld et al., 2019), *ImageNet-Wiki* leads to almost a 12 pp. improvement (38.63% vs. 50.50%) in top-5 accuracy on ImageNet *mp500* test split, which is far higher than achieved in any prior work. These

[1] The dataset, code and trained models available at: `https://bujwid.eu/p/zsl-imagenet-wiki`

Proceedings of the Third Workshop on Beyond Vision and LANguage: inTEgrating Real-world kNowledge (LANTERN), pages 38–52
Kyiv, Ukraine (Online), April 20, 2021

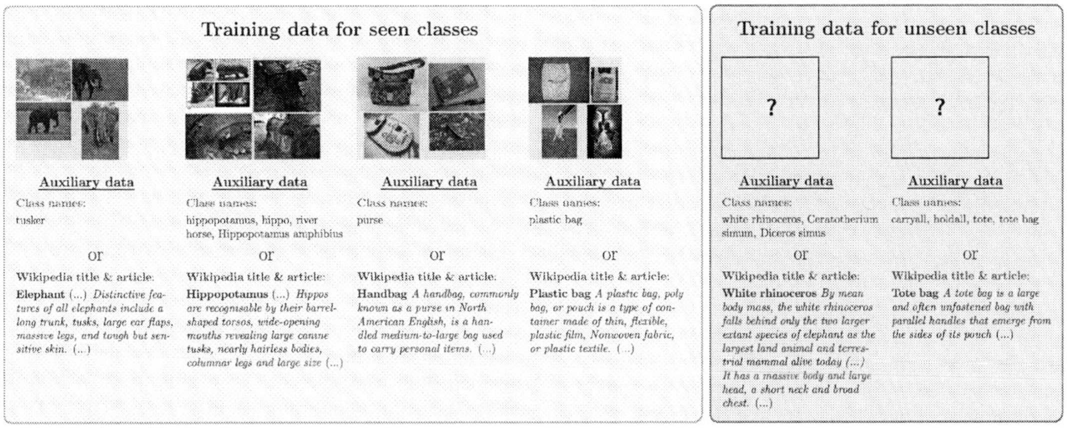

Figure 1: **ImageNet classes and their corresponding auxiliary data: Wikipedia articles or class names.** Above illustrates the difference between class names, the standard source of auxiliary data used on ImageNet, and the textual descriptions we collected. The short, selected article fragments shown contain information that is visually discriminative for the classes. In ZSL, for seen classes, we have access to both auxiliary data and images. However, for unseen classes only auxiliary data is available for training, with no images.

Table 1: **High-level overview of the most popular existing zero-shot learning image datasets.** Numbers with (*) correspond only to the training set only. Provided by: (†) - Reed et al. (2016); (‡) - Elhoseiny et al. (2017).

Dataset	# images	# classes	Used auxiliary data			Semantic classes
			Other	Wiki articles	Attrib.	
aP/aY	15k	32			✓	person, animals, objects
AwA1	30k	50			✓	animals
AwA2	37k	50			✓	animals
LAD	78k	230			✓	animals, fruits, objects, other
SUN	14k	717			✓	scenes
CUB	11k	200	short image capts. (†)	✓(‡)	✓	birds
NABirds	48k	1,011		✓(‡)	✓	birds
ImageNet-Wiki	1.3M*	1,000*	class names	✓(this work)		animals, plants, objects, other

results strongly suggest that algorithmic development on ZSL models is not sufficient for further substantial progress. It is necessary to also consider the quality and type of auxiliary data used. Fortunately, creating or collecting already available textual information about classes is practical, viable, and much less labor-intensive than collecting and annotating images with labels or attributes. Our second main observation is that, regardless of the type of auxiliary data used, ZSL models generalize poorly from one large class category to another. For example, excluding all animal classes from the training set leads to large performance drops on animal species in the test set. Therefore, the field's algorithmic progress measured on small datasets with few categories (Table 1) might not be well aligned with the end goal of using ZSL to scale image classifiers to diverse sets of unseen classes from many diverse categories. Though textual descriptions are already available for smaller datasets (CUB, NABirds) we believe *ImageNet-Wiki* will facilitate further research in this area.

The textual descriptions for ZSL lead to significant performance improvements, but they also have several theoretical and practical advantages over other types of auxiliary data, as we detail in Table 2. Moreover, we believe a large-scale zero-shot learning setup with rich and diverse textual descriptions can be a useful for studying general multimodal machine learning, specifically on the interaction between language and vision. This is because the task is challenging and requires effective modeling of the interaction between modalities for better-than-random accuracy (unlike say VQA where relying on language priors may be possible (Zhang et al., 2016; Goyal et al., 2017)). Additionally, *ImageNet-*

Table 2: Advantages and disadvantages of different auxiliary data types for zero-shot image classification.

Auxiliary data type	Advantages / Disadvantages
Attributes	+ *Little noise*: attributes selected by experts + *Potentially highly discriminative*: depending on the selected features, might be highly informative – *Difficult to scale*: as the number of classes increases, the more attributes are required to discriminate – *Simple relations*: attributes may be conditional and difficult to quantify (e.g. zebra has brown and white stripes at birth) – *Expensive annotation*: requires domain knowledge to define discriminative attributes – *Low flexibility*: difficult to aggregate multiple independent datasets as attributes not standardized
Word embedding of class names	+ *Very simple approach*: little or no labor required to create data – *Sensitive to linguistic issues*: names may partially overlap or not reflect well semantic similarity – *Little information*: the name gives little discriminability of classes
Text descriptions	+ *Rich in information*: likely to be discriminative + *Easy to collect*: many existing resources + *Easy aggregation*: allows conceptually easy aggregation of text from multiple sources – *High noise*: contains non-relevant information

Wiki covers a broad range of many classes, with Wikipedia articles that are long, complex, diverse, and written by many authors. We expect that this experimental setting will lead to more progress as methods become more tailored to relating text language and vision.

Summary of the contributions We demonstrate that simply using better auxiliary data in the form of Wikipedia description of classes outperforms all prior works on zero-shot learning on the *mp500* test split of ImageNet. Additionally, we show ZSL models generalize very poorly to novel super-categories of classes. Finally, we introduce *ImageNet-Wiki*, which provides text from Wikipedia articles of ImageNet classes, which we hope will facilitate the research on ZSL and the interaction between language and vision.

2 Related works

Zero-shot learning The problem of zero-shot learning (ZSL) was initially defined and introduced by Larochelle et al. (2008). A significant fraction of the recent works on ZSL uses attributes as auxiliary data, and small or medium-sized datasets (Xian et al., 2018; Romera-Paredes and Torr, 2015; Changpinyo et al., 2016; Schonfeld et al., 2019). The datasets generally used contain either animal species (CUB, AWA1, AWA2), flower species (Oxford Flower Dataset), or a broader set of classes (SUN, aPY). Some of the works experiment on ImageNet, but due to the lack of attribute annotations, they use word2vec embeddings of class names instead (Xian et al., 2018; Changpinyo et al., 2016; Schonfeld et al., 2019). Creating discriminative attribute annotations becomes more challenging as the number of classes grows, and the differences between classes become more nuanced. We would like the *ImageNet-Wiki* dataset to stimulate future research on large-scale ZSL as it provides a semantically rich source of auxiliary data, shown by our experiments, for ImageNet.

Zero-shot learning from text The portion of ZSL research that is more closely related to our work uses text as auxiliary data. Reed et al. (2016) collected a dataset with multiple single-sentence image-level descriptions for two datasets: CUB-2011 containing bird species and Oxford Flowers dataset with flower species. The general idea of utilizing Wikipedia articles for ZSL has already been studied by Elhoseiny et al. (2016, 2017) on datasets with bird species (CUB-2011, NABirds). The usefulness of such data was more recently additionally supported by Zhu et al. (2018) and Chen et al. (2020). These works were, however, limited to relatively small datasets with only closely related classes compared to ImageNet, which is a much larger dataset and covers a more diverse set of classes.

3 ImageNet–Wikipedia correspondences

ImageNet classes correspond to a subset of synsets representing nouns in WordNet 3.0. Each class is defined by its wnid (WordNet ID), class phrases (which we also refer to as *class names* in this paper), and a gloss (brief description), for example (n02129165; "lion, king of beasts, Panthera leo"; *large gregarious predatory feline of Africa and India having a tawny coat with a shaggy mane in the male*). The synsets have a hierarchical structure, such that our example class is a descendant of classes like "big cat" and "animal".

We create an automatic matching of ImageNet classes to their corresponding Wikipedia pages.[2] The matching is based on the similarity between the synset *words* and Wikipedia titles, as well as their ancestor categories. Unfortunately, such matching occasionally produces false-positives, as it is a difficult problem. One reason for this could be that classes with similar names might represent very different concepts – e.g. (n02389026; "sorrel"; *a horse of a brownish orange to light brown color*) with the herb called "sorrel". To ensure high-quality correspondences in *ImageNet-Wiki*, we first compared all automatic correspondences from both Niemann and Gurevych (2011) and Matuschek and Gurevych (2013), then also manually verified all the matches, and modified them if necessary. The quality of the automatic matches often depends more, for example, on how irrelevant articles are filtered out than on the exact matching approach taken. We refer the interested reader to the source code we provide for the full details.

4 Encoding textual descriptions for zero-shot learning

The text for each class is encoded into a single feature vector. Having features of fixed dimensionality for each class allows us to use standard ZSL approaches. As text encoders we use either ALBERT (Lan et al., 2019), which is an NLP model based on Transformer (Vaswani et al., 2017), or word embeddings models: GloVe (Pennington et al., 2014) or word2vec (Mikolov et al., 2013).

For ALBERT we consider two official pre-trained models: ALBERT-base and ALBERT-xxlarge, which have hidden layer sizes of 768 and 4096 respectively. ALBERT (Lan et al., 2019), similarly to its predecessor BERT (Devlin et al., 2019), uses learnable positional encoding, which has fixed size. Therefore in order to encode pages that can be longer than the maximal length, we split the text into partially overlapping sequences of 256 tokens with an overlap of 50 tokens. We encode each of the sequences with ALBERT, and average the hidden states from the last layer over each token. Such representations of all the sequences are then also averaged to get the final feature vector. We compared alternative ways to extract features in Appendix E.

For word embedding models, either GloVe (Pennington et al., 2014) or word2vec (Mikolov et al., 2013), we use official pre-trained weights. To encode the text we simply embed each token and then average the embedding features over the whole sequence. Finally, if a class has multiple corresponding articles, we average the representations obtained from each of them.

5 Experiments

To compare the quality of different types of auxiliary data, we run experiments on two existing ZSL models. We choose to run all experiments on the standard ZSL task, instead of generalized ZSL (GZSL). That means we predict only unseen classes and not the union between seen and unseen classes. Although GZLS is the more practical long-term scenario, the standard ZSL setup better isolates the usefulness and discriminativeness of auxiliary data from the model's level of overfitting to the seen classes. As we introduce no new methods and focus on the importance of auxiliary data instead, the standards ZSL setup is more informative in our case.

5.1 Zero-shot learning models

We run experiments with a state-of-the-art CADA-VAE (Schonfeld et al., 2019) model. Although it was initially proposed for GZSL, we found that it also works well for the standard ZSL setup. To compare the relative importance of the quality of the model vs. the quality of information contained in auxiliary data, the second model we use is a simple approach based on linear projections. We refer to it as *Simple ZSL*.

CADA-VAE (Schonfeld et al., 2019) The model is based on two Variational Auto-Encoders (VAEs) (Diederik et al., 2014) - one for image features and another for auxiliary data. It aligns the latent spaces of the two VAEs, such that the latent features of an image encoded with the image feature VAE and its class features encoded with auxiliary data VAE should be close to each other. After training the VAEs, a linear classifier is trained from the latent space vectors, obtained from the text description of the unseen classes, to the class labels of

[2]We use enwiki-20200120 dump from `https://dumps.wikimedia.org/backup-index.html` (Accessed: 22 Jan 2020).

these unseen classes.[3] At test time the latent space features obtained from the image VAE are passed to the classifier. We use our own implementation of the model which yields similar results to those reported in the original paper. The details can be found in Appendix F, along with a discussion on the small differences between our and the original implementation.

Simple ZSL model We also create a simple zero-shot learning model inspired by DeViSE (Frome et al., 2013). Unlike the original work, we do not fine-tune the visual model and use two separate linear transformations for image features and auxiliary data to map the different modalities to a joint embedding space. The transformations are trained using a hinge loss which is defined: Assume there are K classes and $\mathbf{x}$ is the visual feature representation of a sample with class label $1 \leq y \leq K$ then the loss is

$$\sum_{\substack{i=1 \\ i \neq y}}^{K} \max\left(0, m - \phi_x(\mathbf{x})^T \phi_t(\mathbf{t}_y) + \phi_x(\mathbf{x})^T \phi_t(\mathbf{t}_i)\right) \tag{1}$$

where $\mathbf{t}_i$ is the feature vector for the auxiliary data of class i, $m \geq 0$ is a scalar corresponding to the margin, $\phi_x(\mathbf{x}) = W_x \mathbf{x} + \mathbf{b}_x$ and $\phi_t(\mathbf{t}_i) = W_t \mathbf{t}_i + \mathbf{b}_t$. Then $W_x, W_t, \mathbf{b}_x$ and $\mathbf{b}_t$ are the trainable parameters in the model. At test time, to classify samples, we use the nearest neighbors between projected visual features and text labels.

5.2 Experimental setup

Our textual descriptions are assessed by comparing them to using word2vec embeddings (Mikolov et al., 2013) of class names as the auxiliary data provided by Changpinyo et al. (2016). The latter is a standard feature used in zero-shot learning on ImageNet (Xian et al., 2018, 2019; Schonfeld et al., 2019). These word2vec representations were also learned on Wikipedia data. However, this is different from encoding explicit textual descriptions of classes.

Data We use standard splits between ImageNet classes proposed by Xian et al. (2018). The *train* and *val* splits consist of 750 and 250 classes, which contain images from ILSVRC-2012 (Russakovsky et al., 2015). Even though the original setup consists of multiple sets of separate test classes, we only use one of them: *mp500* - the 500 most populated classes. We leave studying other splits for future work since it requires providing the corresponding Wikipedia articles for the additional classes in those splits.

Features To represent images we use the 2048-dimensional features provided by Xian et al. (2018), which come from the last layer of a ResNet-101 before pooling. The model was pre-trained on ILSVRC 2012 part of ImageNet, which corresponds to the *trainval* ZSL split we use. Word2vec vector features of ImageNet class names (refered to as word2vec*) are from Changpinyo et al. (2016) have 500-dimensions and were trained on Wikipedia data. These are standard features used on ImageNet and were used by all the models we compare against. For encoding the article text with word2vec, we instead use standard pre-trained 300-dimensional vectors provided by Mikolov et al. (2013). GloVe features are also 300-dimensional and are from Pennington et al. (2014). In all the experiments, we keep both image and auxiliary features fixed.

Choice of the hyper-parameters The hyperparameter values of the models are selected independently for each model and type of auxiliary data feature. The models are trained on the set of *train* classes and their performance evaluated on the *val* classes. We use both random and manual searches over possible settings, and the same number of runs was made on each model variant. More details are in Appendix F. The *val* set consists of a subset of classes that were used to train the image feature extractor, which violates ZSL assumptions. Although that is likely to lead to over-optimistic numbers, *val* performance is used only for the hyperparameter selection.

Evaluation We evaluate the models using the mean per class top-1 and top-5 accuracy which are standard ZSL metrics. All the hyperparameter values used for evaluation on *mp500* set were solely determined based on *val* performance of the models. For the final evaluation, we train the models on *train+val* with 1000 classes (750 *train* + 250 *val*) and use separate 500 classes from *mp500* for measuring performance. Since *ImageNet-Wiki* contains auxiliary features for 489 out of 500 classes from *mp500*, unless stated differently, for a fair com-

[3]This describes the ZSL setting. Originally for GZSL, the latent features from the image samples are also used.

parison, we compute the accuracies of the models using Wikipedia articles assuming 0 accuracy on the remaining classes.

5.3 Results

Comparison of different auxiliary data encodings First, in Table 3, we compare ways to encode the auxiliary data on the *val* set only. We observe that using the whole Wiki articles works better than using just the abstracts (first paragraphs of the articles before any section starts). Also, word embedding encoding of the text appears to work better than the more complex ALBERT model (Lan et al., 2019) with GloVe (Pennington et al., 2014) being the best feature extractor. For completeness of the comparison, we also try to encode class names with ALBERT and GloVe, although ALBERT was designed to work with longer sequences, therefore it can perform poorly with simple class names.

Table 3: **Validation set comparison of different textual inputs and encodings for zero-shot learning on ImageNet**. 750 *train* classes were used as seen and 250 *val* classes as unseen. Hyperparameters for each features type were tuned only on Wiki article data. All ALBERT encodings are of type ALBERT (xxlarge). word2vec* refers to the features provided by Xian et al. (2018) typically used for ZSL, which are different from the standard pretrained word2vec model.

		Result on val	
Auxiliary data	**Features**	top-1 (%)	top-5 (%)
Wiki article	GloVe	**40.24**	**77.96**
Wiki article	word2vec	36.14	72.80
Wiki article	ALBERT	31.29	64.92
Wiki abstract	ALBERT	22.71	52.84
Class names	ALBERT	14.19	30.53
Gloss	ALBERT	19.67	48.09
Class names & gloss	ALBERT	21.38	49.75
Class names	GloVe	29.47	59.26
Gloss	GloVe	22.41	54.91
Class names & gloss	GloVe	33.26	65.47
Class names*	word2vec*	27.87	61.91

Evaluating models and feature types on the test set In Table 4, we compare zero-shot learning accuracies of various models on the *mp500* test split. Our experiments compare two different types of auxiliary information, class names encoded with word2vec, which is a standard approach on ImageNet, as well as using Wikipedia articles that we extract, encoded with two variants of ALBERT and two variants of word embedding encodings. The results show that models using the textual descriptions consistently achieve higher accuracies. The increased performance is even more prominent on the simple ZSL model. When using textual descriptions, such a simple model outperforms much more complex and generally better CADA-VAE trained with word2vec features of class names. This demonstrates not only the high quality of information the Wikipedia articles convey about the classes but also that the information can be effectively extracted even by simple models. In Figure 2, we additionally compare the results we achieve with those reported by Xian et al. (2018) of different zero-shot learning methods. The general setup we used is the same and uses the same image features, data splits and word2vec vectors of the class names. The comparison demonstrates that the models using Wikipedia articles outperform all the prior methods, highlighting the relative impor-

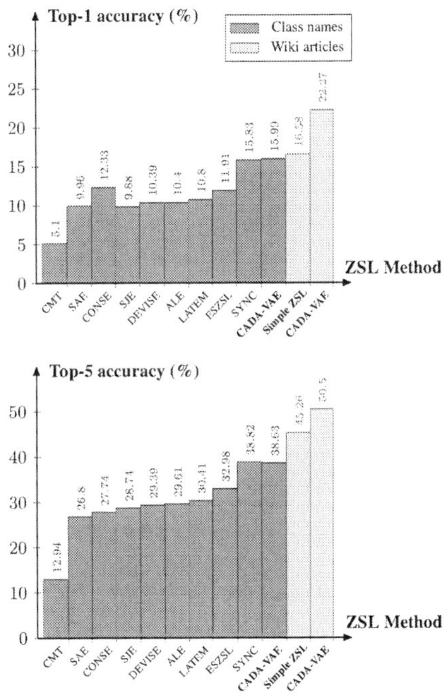

Figure 2: Reported results for zero-shot learning on the ImageNet dataset and the mp500 test split. Color indicates the auxiliary data type used. Methods in boldface correspond to the implementations in our paper, the other numbers were reported by Xian et al. (2018). We chose the best performing variants of our models from Table 4.

Table 4: Zero-shot learning results of the models we evaluate on ImageNet dataset. word2vec* uses features from Changpinyo et al. (2016) and is different from word2vec which are standard pre-trained vectors. We report the mean and standard deviation values from 5 training runs with different random seeds.

Model	Auxiliary data	Features	Result on mp500	
			top-1 (%)	top-5 (%)
CADA-VAE (Schonfeld et al., 2019)	class names	word2vec*	15.99 ± 0.25	38.63 ± 0.43
CADA-VAE (Schonfeld et al., 2019)	Wiki articles	ALBERT (base)	17.04 ± 0.13	40.23 ± 0.27
CADA-VAE (Schonfeld et al., 2019)	Wiki articles	ALBERT (xxlarge)	18.84 ± 0.21	43.94 ± 0.24
CADA-VAE (Schonfeld et al., 2019)	Wiki articles	word2vec	20.34 ± 0.31	47.50 ± 0.01
CADA-VAE (Schonfeld et al., 2019)	Wiki articles	GloVe	$\mathbf{22.27 \pm 0.20}$	$\mathbf{50.50 \pm 0.33}$
Simple ZSL	class names	word2vec*	9.08 ± 0.18	27.31 ± 0.23
Simple ZSL	Wiki articles	ALBERT (base)	13.91 ± 0.23	37.31 ± 0.18
Simple ZSL	Wiki articles	ALBERT (xxlarge)	$\mathbf{16.60 \pm 0.08}$	42.39 ± 0.30
Simple ZSL	Wiki articles	word2vec	14.84 ± 0.24	42.93 ± 0.20
Simple ZSL	Wiki articles	GloVe	$\mathbf{16.58 \pm 0.19}$	$\mathbf{45.26 \pm 0.24}$

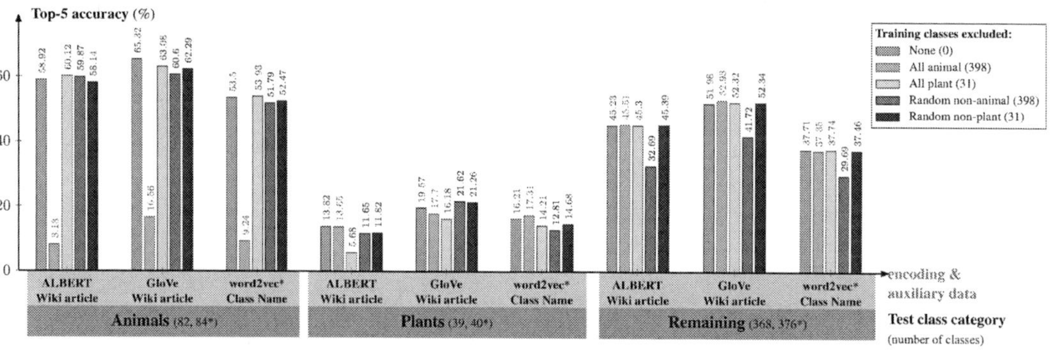

Figure 3: **Within and across category generalization of ZSL. Top-5 per class accuracy on CADA-VAE.** We show the effect of excluding a category of classes from the training set on ZSL performance for all mp500 test set categories. Specifically we compare excluding all *animal* classes vs. excluding the same number of random *non-animal* classes. We repeat the same process for the *plant* class. Different models trained on different auxiliary data are compared. The performance numbers are from a single run each. The performance on the unseen *animal* classes drops dramatically when the animal classes are removed from the training set, the red bars in the first grouping of plots. The same trend, though not as pronounced, can be seen for the *remaining* classes, the gray bars in the last grouping of plots. The number of test classes is slightly higher for models using class name data (marked with *) since Wiki articles are missing for some classes.

tance of the auxiliary data type and algorithmic development.

Generalization outside the seen groups of classes The hierarchical structure of WordNet entities, used as ImageNet classes, allows us to study different groups of classes separately. In Figure 3, we split the set of both train and test classes into three disjoint partitions: *animals*, *plants*, and *remaining* and compare the test performance on all subgroups when some of them are excluded from the training set. First of all, the performance on *plants* is generally much lower than the much more populated *animals* group. Moreover, we see that all the models have poor accuracy on *animals* when that group is excluded from the training set. These results show the models' inability to generalize to unseen classes that are semantically far from seen classes. Therefore, they also suggest that studying ZSL on ImageNet might be more practical than datasets with a less diverse set of classes.

Analyzing the impact of class similarity Even though ImageNet classes represent distinct concepts, since WordNet and Wikipedia were created independently, naturally, the granularity of the concepts they define can be different. As a consequence, some of the classes can be mapped to multiple articles. For example, class (n02965783, "car mirror") was assigned two more detailed articles:

Table 5: **Performance on subsets of mp500 that excludes classes that are similar to those in the training set.** We take two CADA-VAE models (single runs), trained to predict all unseen classes and present their mean per-class accuracies of different subsets of the *mp500* classes. Test classes are excluded based on their overlap with the train+val classes in either: Wikipedia pages correspondences or WordNet phrases (defining the classes). Each row corresponds to a different subset of excluded classes. Examples of excluded classes are: **Row 3**: (n03792972, "mountain tent") is removed as train+val contains (n02769963, "backpacking tent", "pack tent") and all are mapped to "Tent". **Row 4**: (n04543772, "wagon wheel") is removed as it maps to ["Wagon", "Wheel"], and class (n02974003, "car wheel") in train+val maps to "Wheel". **Row 5**: (n03222516, "doorbell, bell, buzzer") is removed as there is (n03017168, "chime, bell, gong") in train+val. The numbers shown in bold display the results with the biggest drop in performance.

		ALBERT-xxlarge Wiki articles		GloVe Wiki articles		word2vec class names	
Classes excluded	**# classes left**	top-1 (%)	top-5 (%)	top-1 (%)	top-5 (%)	top-1 (%)	top-5 (%)
None	500	18.73	44.03	22.26	50.49	16.38	39.07
No matching articles	489	19.16	45.02	22.76	51.63	16.28	39.00
Same set of articles matched (*)	459	16.82	42.63	21.08	49.82	16.18	39.04
(Any) article overlap	439	**15.07**	**40.64**	**19.87**	**48.38**	15.68	38.60
Class names overlap (†)	463	18.24	44.50	21.99	51.31	**15.53**	**38.05**
(*) ∪ (†)	438	16.39	42.42	20.79	49.76	15.70	38.35

"Rear-view mirror", "Wing mirror". In fact, WordNet synsets used as ImageNet classes consist of one or more (closely related) concepts that are considered equivalent. On the other hand, two different classes can be assigned the same set of articles. Potential overlap of sources of auxiliary information (Wiki pages or class phrases) can be present due to a high degree of similarity between corresponding classes, or compound classes being defined on other classes (e.g. *wagon wheel* being a *wheel* of a *wagon*). This phenomenon is associated not only with the particular auxiliary data we propose. As we observe in Table 5, models using both sources of data have lower performance on subsets of test classes which exclude those that are similar to the training classes under various criteria defined for those types of auxiliary data. As shown in the last row, the model using Wikipedia text still outperforms the one using class phrases on the subset of test classes that exclude those that are similar to training classes in either Wikipedia pages or class phrases. However, as demonstrated in our results in Figure 3, certain degree of similarity between seen and unseen classes is necessary for reasonable performance.

Qualitative evaluation of prediction To provide further insight into models' performance, we analyze confusion matrices with predictions of different models. Due to the immense size, the full confusion matrices are included only in the supplementary material. Figure 4 shows only a selected subset of the confusion matrices, only with classes that were often confused. The mispredictions are mainly within relatively semantically similar classes – different types of furniture in this case. Generally, the pattern for models using Wiki articles seems more diagonal, with more values close to 0. This suggests that Wiki articles are richer in discriminative information. More figures are available in Appendix C.

Text length vs. performance Finally, we also analyse the impact of the length of textual descriptions of classes and performance on them. Longer descriptions tend to lead to higher accuracy. The trend is not strong, however. The details are discussed in Appendix B.

6 Limitations & future work

The performance of our approach is likely to depend on some general quality of Wikipedia articles. Although we have not evaluated this dependence directly in our work, at least the article's length indeed correlates with the corresponding class's accuracy (Appendix B). Therefore, the adaptability of the general approach to some particular domains not well-covered in Wikipedia can also be limited. Additionally, we assume that the classes used are possible to match with Wikipedia articles. With

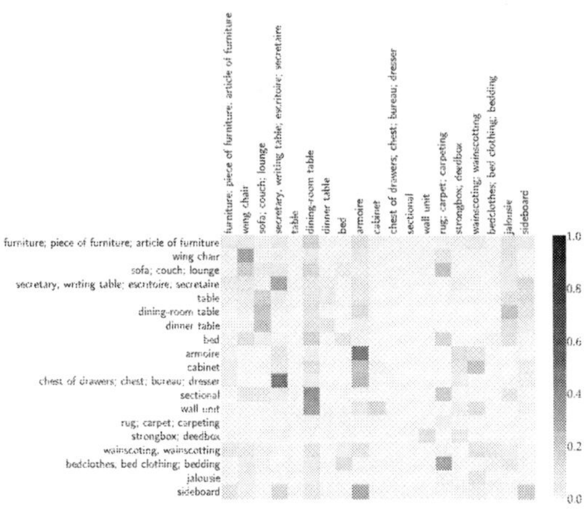

(a) word2vec - class names

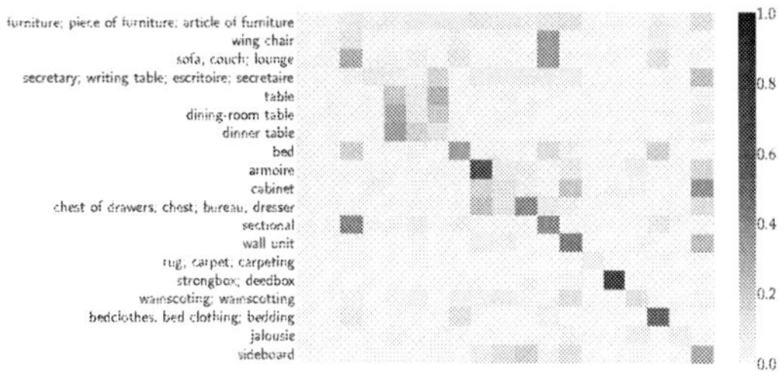

(b) GloVe - Wiki articles

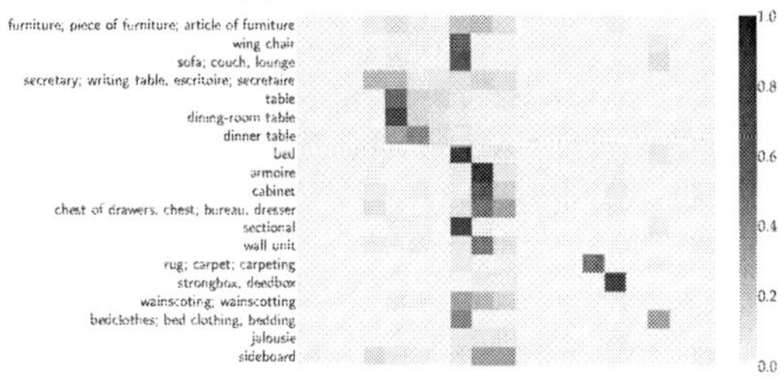

(c) ALBERT-xxlarge - Wiki articles

Figure 4: **A selected subset of confusion matrices on mp500 test set.** All the models are CADA-VAE (Schonfeld et al., 2019) trained on different types of auxiliary data. The rows correspond to true labels, columns to predicted classes - the matrices are row-normalized. The subset of classes was selected by choosing one class and including others that were the most frequently mutually confused by any of the models.

very few exceptions, this is true for the ImageNet classes we consider. However, it is possible to find cases where this would not be possible due to the different granularities of the classes and Wikipedia pages.

The ZSL methods we use can utilize the information from our textual descriptions effectively, however, they only rely on features from pretrained, off-the-shelf models. Given that the textual descriptions are complex and contain only a sparse amount of visually relevant information, future research is needed to find methods more effective at fully utilizing our textual descriptions. Additionally, there is a potential of using our textual descriptions for different purposes, such as pretraining of image recognition models, similarly to the recent works by Desai and Johnson (2020) and Radford et al. (2021). Finally, the issue of generalization to groups of classes remains an open challenge.

7 Conclusions

We demonstrate that simply employing Wikipedia articles as auxiliary data for ZSL on ImageNet yields a state-of-the-art performance, even on a relatively weak model. Additionally, we show that standard ZSL models poorly generalize across categories of classes. Finally, we share the *ImageNet-Wiki* dataset with Wikipedia articles describing corresponding ImageNet classes to facilitate further the research on ZSL, as well as on the interaction between language and vision more generally.

Acknowledgments

This work was supported by the Wallenberg AI, Autonomous Systems and Software Program (WASP) funded by the Knut and Alice Wallenberg Foundation.

References

Soravit Changpinyo, Wei-Lun Chao, Boqing Gong, and Fei Sha. 2016. Synthesized classifiers for zero-shot learning. In *Proceedings of the Conference on Computer Vision and Pattern Recognition (CVPR)*.

Zhi Chen, Jingjing Li, Yadan Luo, Zi Huang, and Yang Yang. 2020. Canzsl: Cycle-consistent adversarial networks for zero-shot learning from natural language. In *Proceedings of the IEEE/CVF Winter Conference on Applications of Computer Vision*, pages 874–883.

Karan Desai and Justin Johnson. 2020. Virtex: Learning visual representations from textual annotations. *arXiv preprint arXiv:2006.06666*.

Jacob Devlin, Ming-Wei Chang, Kenton Lee, and Kristina Toutanova. 2019. Bert: Pre-training of deep bidirectional transformers for language understanding. In *Proceedings of the 2019 Conference of the North American Chapter of the Association for Computational Linguistics: Human Language Technologies, Volume 1 (Long and Short Papers)*, pages 4171–4186.

P Kingma Diederik, Max Welling, et al. 2014. Auto-encoding variational bayes. In *Proceedings of the International Conference on Learning Representations (ICLR)*, volume 1.

Mohamed Elhoseiny, Ahmed Elgammal, and Babak Saleh. 2016. Write a classifier: Predicting visual classifiers from unstructured text. *IEEE Transactions on Pattern Analysis and Machine Intelligence (TPAMI)*, 39(12):2539–2553.

Mohamed Elhoseiny, Yizhe Zhu, Han Zhang, and Ahmed Elgammal. 2017. Link the head to the" beak": Zero shot learning from noisy text description at part precision. In *Proceedings of the Conference on Computer Vision and Pattern Recognition (CVPR)*.

Andrea Frome, Greg S Corrado, Jon Shlens, Samy Bengio, Jeff Dean, Marc'Aurelio Ranzato, and Tomas Mikolov. 2013. Devise: A deep visual-semantic embedding model. In *Advances in Neural Information Processing Systems (NIPS)*.

Yash Goyal, Tejas Khot, Douglas Summers-Stay, Dhruv Batra, and Devi Parikh. 2017. Making the V in VQA matter: Elevating the role of image understanding in Visual Question Answering. In *Conference on Computer Vision and Pattern Recognition (CVPR)*.

Zhenzhong Lan, Mingda Chen, Sebastian Goodman, Kevin Gimpel, Piyush Sharma, and Radu Soricut. 2019. Albert: A lite bert for self-supervised learning of language representations. In *International Conference on Learning Representations*.

Hugo Larochelle, Dumitru Erhan, and Yoshua Bengio. 2008. Zero-data learning of new tasks. In *Proceedings of the 23rd national conference on Artificial intelligence-Volume 2*, pages 646–651.

Michael Matuschek and Iryna Gurevych. 2013. Dijkstra-wsa: A graph-based approach to word sense alignment. *Transactions of the Association for Computational Linguistics*, 1:151–164.

Tomas Mikolov, Ilya Sutskever, Kai Chen, Greg S Corrado, and Jeff Dean. 2013. Distributed representations of words and phrases and their compositionality. In *Advances in neural information processing systems*, pages 3111–3119.

Elisabeth Niemann and Iryna Gurevych. 2011. The people's web meets linguistic knowledge: automatic sense alignment of wikipedia and wordnet. In *Proceedings of the Ninth International Conference on Computational Semantics*, pages 205–214. Association for Computational Linguistics.

Jeffrey Pennington, Richard Socher, and Christopher D Manning. 2014. Glove: Global vectors for word representation. In *Proceedings of the 2014 conference on empirical methods in natural language processing (EMNLP)*, pages 1532–1543.

Alec Radford, Jong Wook Kim, Chris Hallacy, Aditya Ramesh, Gabriel Goh, Sandhini Agarwal, Girish Sastry, Amanda Askell, Pamela Mishkin, Jack Clark, et al. 2021. Learning transferable visual models from natural language supervision.

Scott Reed, Zeynep Akata, Honglak Lee, and Bernt Schiele. 2016. Learning deep representations of fine-grained visual descriptions. In *Proceedings of the IEEE Conference on Computer Vision and Pattern Recognition*, pages 49–58.

Bernardino Romera-Paredes and Philip Torr. 2015. An embarrassingly simple approach to zero-shot learning. In *Proceedings of the International Conference on Machine Learning (ICML)*.

Olga Russakovsky, Jia Deng, Hao Su, Jonathan Krause, Sanjeev Satheesh, Sean Ma, Zhiheng Huang, Andrej Karpathy, Aditya Khosla, Michael Bernstein, et al. 2015. Imagenet large scale visual recognition challenge. *International journal of computer vision*, 115(3):211–252.

Edgar Schonfeld, Sayna Ebrahimi, Samarth Sinha, Trevor Darrell, and Zeynep Akata. 2019. Generalized zero-and few-shot learning via aligned variational autoencoders. In *Proceedings of the IEEE Conference on Computer Vision and Pattern Recognition*, pages 8247–8255.

Ashish Vaswani, Noam Shazeer, Niki Parmar, Jakob Uszkoreit, Llion Jones, Aidan N Gomez, Łukasz Kaiser, and Illia Polosukhin. 2017. Attention is all you need. In *Advances in neural information processing systems*, pages 5998–6008.

Yongqin Xian, Christoph H Lampert, Bernt Schiele, and Zeynep Akata. 2018. Zero-shot learning—a comprehensive evaluation of the good, the bad and the ugly. *IEEE transactions on pattern analysis and machine intelligence*, 41(9):2251–2265.

Yongqin Xian, Saurabh Sharma, Bernt Schiele, and Zeynep Akata. 2019. f-vaegan-d2: A feature generating framework for any-shot learning. In *Proceedings of the IEEE Conference on Computer Vision and Pattern Recognition*, pages 10275–10284.

Peng Zhang, Yash Goyal, Douglas Summers-Stay, Dhruv Batra, and Devi Parikh. 2016. Yin and Yang: Balancing and answering binary visual questions. In *Conference on Computer Vision and Pattern Recognition (CVPR)*.

Yizhe Zhu, Mohamed Elhoseiny, Bingchen Liu, Xi Peng, and Ahmed Elgammal. 2018. A generative adversarial approach for zero-shot learning from noisy texts. In *Proceedings of the IEEE conference on computer vision and pattern recognition*, pages 1004–1013.

A Broader Impact

We anticipate that the dataset we share will make research on multimodal machine learning more accessible, especially to research communities with fewer resources available. More speculatively, we hope that in the future, work on incorporating information from multiple modalities could potentially contribute towards progress on the robustness and flexibility of machine learning models.

We would also like to point out the potential risk of the models reinforcing biases present in sources of text, in particular, in the data we use. The authors of Wikipedia generally represent a very non-diverse social group.[4] Moreover, the content of the database has been shown to contain biases, including the selection of topics it covers.[5] This challenge could potentially be mitigated to some degree with more research progress on interpretable machine learning and bias reduction methods.

[4] https://en.wikipedia.org/wiki/Gender_bias_on_Wikipedia (Accessed: 16 Nov 2020).

[5] https://en.wikipedia.org/wiki/Wikipedia#Coverage_of_topics_and_systemic_bias (Accessed: 16 Nov 2020).

B The effect of text length on accuracy

In Figure 5, we show the relation between the top-5 class accuracy and the length of the textual description of that class. In general, the classes with longer corresponding text tend to yield better accuracy, although the general trend is not strong. However, the impact of the text length appears to be different among different class groups. On animal classes, the relation is negligible. However, on plant classes the relation is much stronger. This observation is especially important since the plant classes generally compose a relatively small fraction of seen classes, and the model has relatively low performance on this group (see Figure 3). This result indicates that using longer textual descriptions can partially mitigate the effect of a group of classes not being well represented in the seen classes.

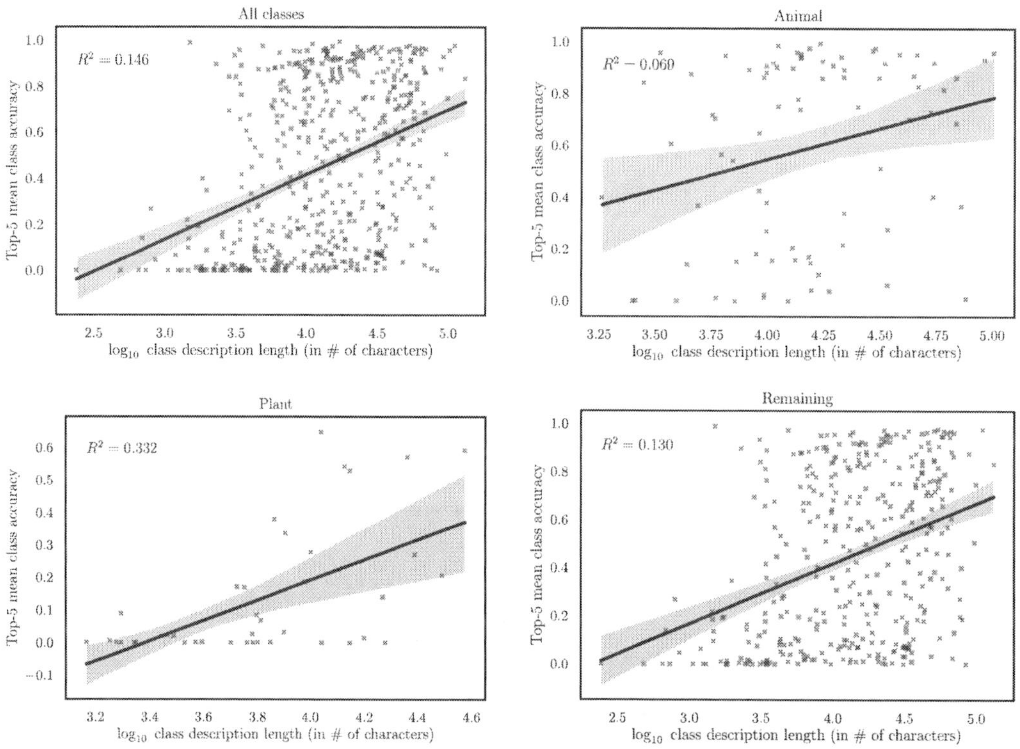

Figure 5: **The relation between the top-5 accuracy on a given class and the length of its Wikipedia pages, separately for different groups of classes from *mp500* test set.** The model used is CADA-VAE trained on the Wikipedia articles using ALBERT-xxlarge features. The lengths are expressed in the $\log_{10}$ of the number of characters. In case a class has more than one page, we sum the lengths of all pages. Note different ranges of axes.

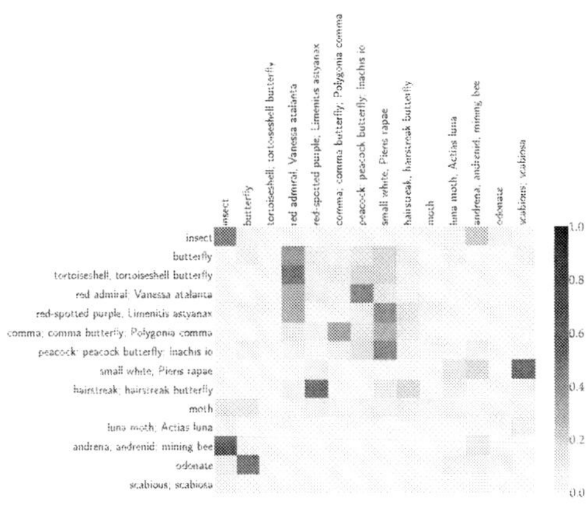

(a) word2vec - class names

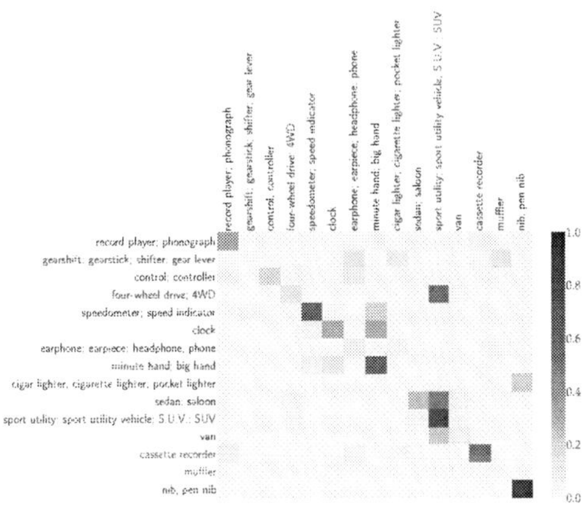

(b) word2vec - class names

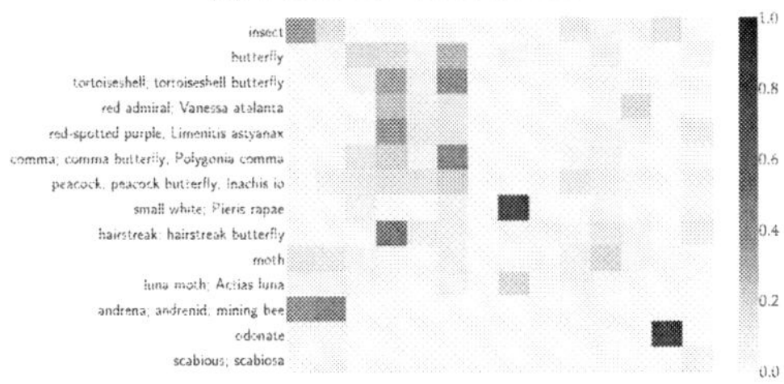

(c) GloVe - Wiki articles

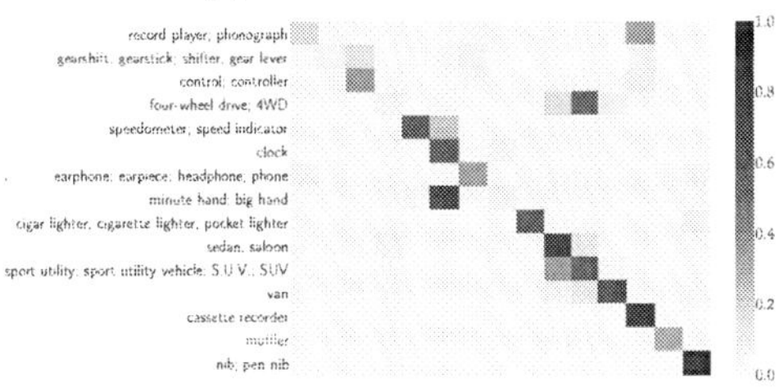

(d) GloVe - Wiki articles

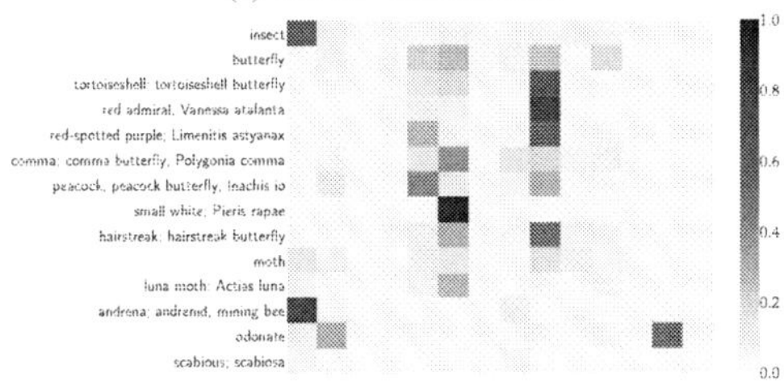

(e) ALBERT-xxlarge - Wiki articles

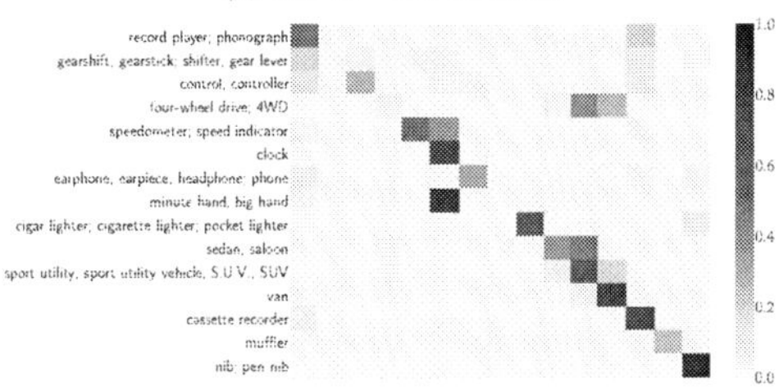

(f) ALBERT-xxlarge - Wiki articles

Figure 6: **Subsets of confusion matrices on mp500 test set.** All the models are CADA-VAE (Schonfeld et al., 2019) trained on different types of auxiliary data. The rows correspond to true labels, columns to predicted classes - the matrices are row-normalized. The subset of classes was selected by choosing one class and including others that were the most frequently mutually confused by any of the models. The general performance differs between different subsets of classes - the pattern is less diagonal on the left than on the right column.

C Additional confusion matrices

In Figure 6, we show confusion matrices for more subsets of classes. On one of the subsets (left), the predictions are generally more noisy. However, the mispredictions generally fall within similar classes (different species of insects on the left side). Additionally, we include the full confusion matrices in the supplementary material as standalone files.

D Additional across-category generalization results

For completeness, in Figure 7, we also show the additional results of models trained on datasets that excluded different groups of classes. The main trend is, however, similar to the observed in Figure 3. We observe that models perform very poorly on animal classes if the training set excluded animals. Additionally, the performance on plant classes is generally lower - likely due to the smaller set of classes in the training set.

E Different ALBERT encodings

Table 6 compares different ways to encode the textual descriptions with ALBERT (Lan et al., 2019), such as how to extract features from individual pages and aggregate the page features for classes with more than one corresponding Wikipedia article. ALBERT (Lan et al., 2019) has a special

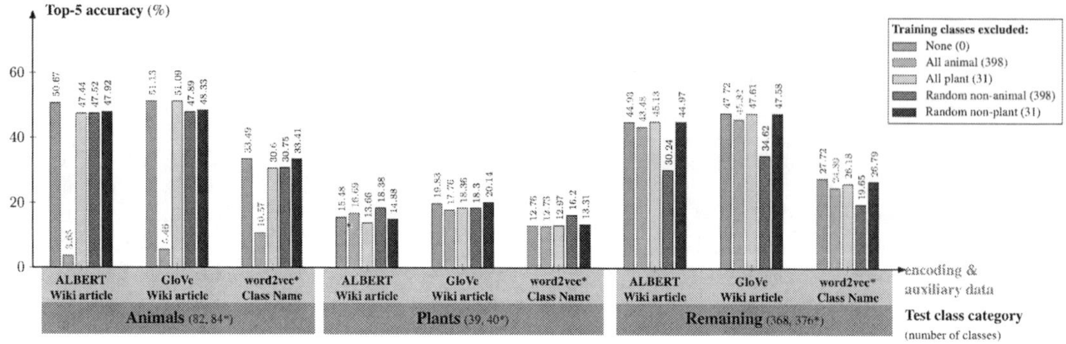

(a) Simple ZSL, Top-5 accuracy

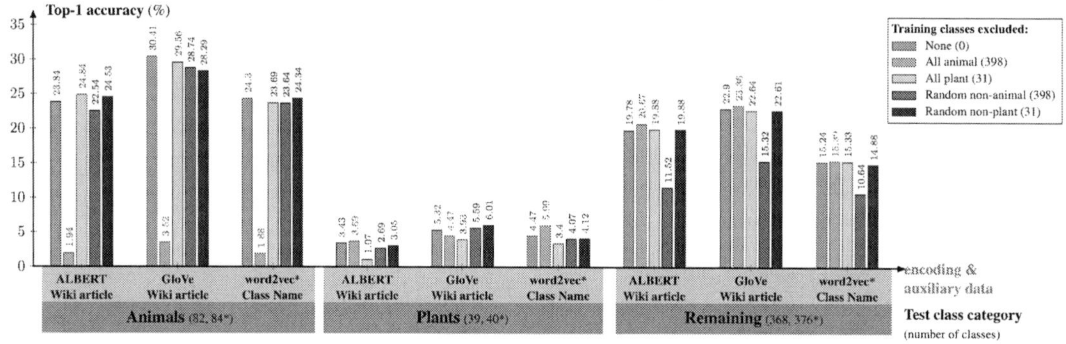

(b) CADA-VAE, Top-1 accuracy

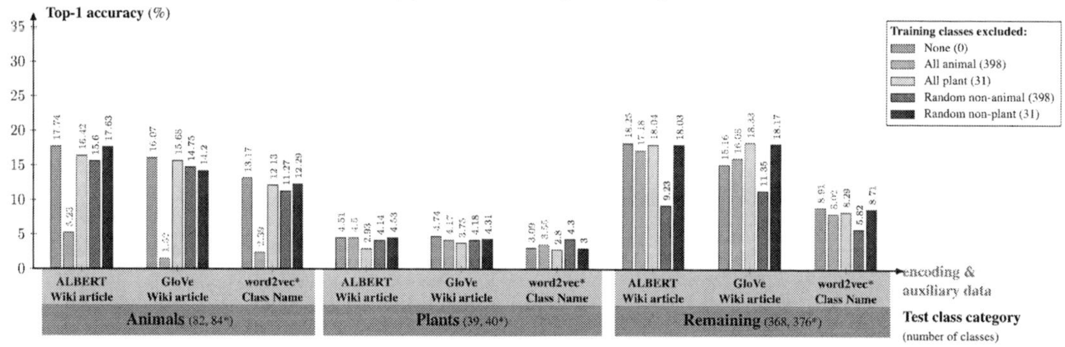

(c) Simple ZSL, Top-1 accuracy

Figure 7: **Within and across category generalization of ZSL.** We show the effect of excluding a category of classes from the training set on ZSL performance for all mp500 test set categories. Specifically we compare excluding all *animal* classes vs. excluding the same number of random *non-animal* classes. We repeat the same process for the *plant* class. Different models trained on different auxiliary data are compared. The performance numbers are from a single run each. The performance on the unseen *animal* classes drops dramatically when the animal classes are removed from the training set, the red bars in the first grouping of plots. The same trend, though not as pronounced, can be seen for the *remaining* classes, the gray bars in the last grouping of plots. The number of test classes is slightly higher for models using class name data (marked with *) since Wiki articles are missing for some classes.

output used for classification ("[CLS]"), which we additionally evaluate for extracting features. However, averaging features over each tokens seem to work much better. Additionally, averaging features among multiple pages works best. All other our experiments use averaging both the page represen-

Table 6: **Validation set comparison of different textual inputs and encodings for zero-shot learning on ImageNet**. The reported metrics are mean per class top-1 and top-5 accuracies of the validation classes. 750 *train* classes were used as seen and 250 *val* classes as unseen. All other hyparameters of Wikipedia models are the same and were chose based on the performance of the model from the first row. The model using class names had hyperparameters tuned independently. [CLS] represents the special output in ALBERT, typically used for classification tasks.

				Result	
Auxiliary data	**Features**	**Page rep.**	**Page aggreg.**	top-1 (%)	top-5 (%)
Wiki articles	ALBERT (xxlarge)	mean tokens	mean	**31.29**	**64.92**
Wiki articles	ALBERT (xxlarge)	mean tokens	sum	29.77	62.44
Wiki articles	ALBERT (xxlarge)	[CLS] output	mean	3.24	12.45
Class names	word2vec	N/A	N/A	27.87	61.91

tations and for aggregating page features (as in row 1, Table 6).

F Model details

F.1 Simple ZSL

We individually tune model hyperparameters for three different types of auxiliary data: class names with word2vec features, Wikipedia articles with either ALBERT-base or ALBERT-xxlarge features. We use Adam optimizer and a random search to generate 40 different hyperparameter settings and choose the best setting for each model variant. The ranges of values used for different hyperparameters were as following: batch size $\in \{32, 128, 256, 512, 1024\}$, target projection dimension defined by the shapes of W_t and $W_x \in \{32, 128, 256, 512, 1024\}$, margin $m \in (0.1, 100.)$ or with equal probability $m = 1$, β_1 (for Adam) $\in \{0.5, 0.9\}$ learning rate $\in (0.00003, 0.01)$. The values are sampled uniformly in the log space of the ranges.

The best configurations of hyperparameter values for each model variant are attached in the supplementary material together with the model weights.

F.2 CADA-VAE

Implementation details We use our own implementation of CADA-VAE [35] and verify that it performs similarly to the original. However, we there are two modification that we do. The official implementation of CADA-VAE[6] appears to incorrectly implement reparameterization trick of Variation Auto-Encoders [11]. It misses the factor of 0.5 when transforming $\log(\sigma^2)$ into σ. Instead, we use $\sigma = \exp(0.5 \cdot \log(\sigma^2))$. Also, unlike the original authors, instead of using a sum to aggregate loss function over samples in a batch, we use a mean. However, this difference should not be important as it can be compensated for by different learning rate or scaling factors of the loss function.

Hyperparameters Like for Simple ZSL, the best values of hyperparameters are chosen individually for each of the three different auxiliary data sources. However, for CADA-VAE we use a combination of manual and random search over hyperparameter values.

The random search consisted of 42 runs on each of the model variant using the following ranges: batch size $\in \{32, 128, 256, 512, 1024\}$, VAE latent space dimension $\in \{32, 128, 256, 512, 1024\}$, VAE image features encoder $\in \{[1560, 1560], [2048, 1024], [1560], [1024, 512]\}$, VAE image features decoder $\in \{[1660], [1024, 2048], [1560], [512]\}$, VAE auxiliary features encoder $\in \{[1560, 1560], [2048, 1024], [1560], [1024, 512]\}$, VAE auxiliary features decoder $\in \{[1660], [1024, 2048], [1560], [2048], [512]\}$, β factor $\in (0.1, 30)$ or with probability 0.3 fixed $\beta = 1$, cross reconstruction loss factor $\in (0.25, 50.)$, distributional alignment loss factor $\in (0.25, 100.)$. Same as for Simple ZSL, the values were sampled uniformly in the log space of the ranges. The loss function factors were used for linearly increasing loss function coefficients.

[6] https://github.com/edgarschnfld/CADA-VAE-PyTorch

The schedules for the coefficients were the same as in the original work, that is: β (for scaling VAE KL-divergence loss) was increased from epoch 0 to 93 (or fixed $\beta = 1$, cross reconstruction loss from epoch 21 to 75, and distribution alignment from epoch 6 to 22. The rest of the hyperparameters were constant for the random search. We used AMSGrad optimizer, learning rate of VAEs of 0.00015. For the linear classifier we use: learning rate of 0.001, Adam optimizer, batch size of 32 and 200 sampled latent space vectors from each class. Additionally, we tried 58 evaluation runs on the variant using word2vec features, and only a subset of those settings on the models using ALBERT-base (21 runs), or ALBERT-xxlarge (19 runs) features.

The best configurations of hyperparameter values for each model variant are attached in the supplementary material together with the model weights.

What Did This Castle Look Like Before? Exploring Referential Relations in Naturally Occurring Multimodal Texts

Ronja Utescher
Friedrich-Schiller-University Jena/
Bielefeld University
r.utescher@uni-bielefeld.de

Sina Zarrieß
Bielefeld University
sina.zarriess@uni-bielefeld.de

Abstract

Multi-modal texts are abundant and diverse in structure, yet Vision & Language research of these naturally occurring texts has mostly focused on genres that are comparatively light on text, like tweets. In this paper, we discuss the challenges and potential benefits of a V&L framework that explicitly models referential relations, taking Wikipedia articles about buildings as an example. We briefly survey existing related tasks in V&L and propose multi-modal information extraction as a general direction for future research.

1 Introduction

Many types of naturally occuring texts are inherently multi-modal: articles, social media posts, recipes, encyclopedias, manuals, advertisement, comics, etc. Research on semiotics has long noted that the relationship between the linguistic and visual elements of such texts is extremely complex (Hardy-Vallée, 2016) and varies widely across genres (Delin and Bateman, 2002). To date, research in Vision & Language, however, has mostly focussed on crowdsourced data that simply aligns relatively short snippets of text to images (e.g. Wu et al. (2017)), sequences of images (e.g. Yang et al. (2019)) or video (e.g. Pan et al. (2020)). Here, the text-image relationship is simplified to a substantial, if not artificial, degree.

In this paper, we take a qualitative look at some examples of real-world multi-modal texts, i.e. Wikipedia articles on entities of the type "building". We find that many phenomena occuring jointly in these texts are currenlty tackled as separated tasks in V&L or text processing. We argue that a promising direction for future research in V&L is to aim for a joint framework that combines these different phenomena and levels of analysis. We believe that such a framework would be useful in a range of typical NLP applications (such as information extraction) where, currently, state-of-the-art models usually only process the text of a multimodal document. Arnold and Tilton (2020) discuss the motivation for such projects in the context Digital Humanities.

The example documents discussed in this paper differ from typical objects of V&L research in many respects, but most importantly in terms of their (i) structure and (ii) semantics or topic. Thus, our building articles are relatively long (i.e. much longer than image paragraphs in Krause et al. (2017)), contain multiple images and text segments that *do not* directly relate to any of the images. Concerning their semantics, the documents discuss buildings which constitute a type of named entity. This entity can be depicted visually in very diverse ways (see Section 2) and that can be associated with a rich body of knowledge (e.g. historical events) described in the text. We will show how these two aspects call for a V&L framework that accounts for *diverse referential relations* whereas in most V&L tasks assume a single, *fixed* text-image relation.

2 Qualitative Case Study

This section discusses observations we made by manually exploring a range of building articles from Wikipedia. We leave the empirical consolidation of our findings for future work.

2.1 Structure of Referential Relations

We first look at different structural aspects of referential relations in the *Holstentor* article, shown in Fig. 1. The first paragraph contains a general description of the entity, its location, importance etc., and is accompanied by a captioned image on its right side. In parallel to the text, this first image visually introduces the entity of the *Holstentor* but, other than that, has no further relations to paragraph it is aligned with.

Proceedings of the Third Workshop on Beyond Vision and LANguage: inTEgrating Real-world kNowledge (LANTERN), pages 53–60
Kyiv, Ukraine (Online), April 20, 2021

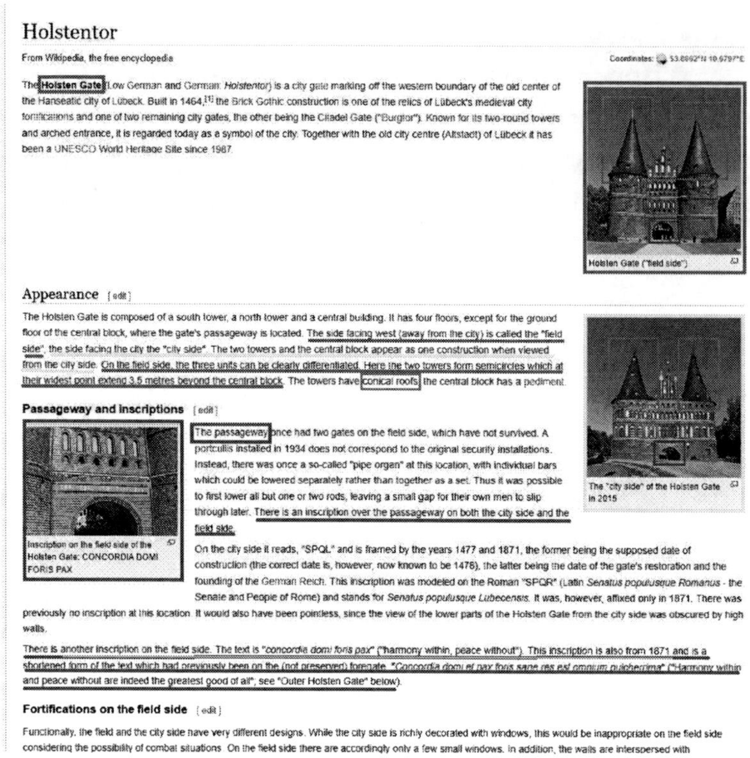

Holstenor

From Wikipedia, the free encyclopedia

Coordinates: 53.8662°N 10.6797°E

The Holsten Gate (Low German and German: *Holstentor*) is a city gate marking off the western boundary of the old center of the Hanseatic city of Lübeck. Built in 1464,[1] the Brick Gothic construction is one of the relics of Lübeck's medieval city fortifications and one of two remaining city gates, the other being the Citadel Gate ("Burgtor"). Known for its two-round towers and arched entrance, it is regarded today as a symbol of the city. Together with the old city centre (Altstadt) of Lübeck it has been a UNESCO World Heritage Site since 1987.

Holsten Gate ("field side")

Appearance [edit]

The Holsten Gate is composed of a south tower, a north tower and a central building. It has four floors, except for the ground floor of the central block, where the gate's passageway is located. The side facing west (away from the city) is called the "field side", the side facing the city the "city side". The two towers and the central block appear as one construction when viewed from the city side. On the field side, the three units can be clearly differentiated. Here the two towers form semicircles which at their widest point extend 3.5 metres beyond the central block. The towers have conical roofs; the central block has a pediment.

The "city side" of the Holsten Gate in 2015

Passageway and inscriptions [edit]

Inscription on the field side of the Holsten Gate: CONCORDIA DOMI FORIS PAX

The passageway once had two gates on the field side, which have not survived. A portcullis installed in 1934 does not correspond to the original security installations. Instead, there was once a so-called "pipe organ" at this location, with individual bars which could be lowered separately rather than together as a set. Thus it was possible to first lower all but one or two rods, leaving a small gap for their own men to slip through later. There is an inscription over the passageway on both the city side and the field side.

On the city side it reads, "SPQL" and is framed by the years 1477 and 1871, the former being the supposed date of construction (the correct date is, however, now known to be 1478), the latter being the date of the gate's restoration and the founding of the German Reich. This inscription was modeled on the Roman "SPQR" (Latin *Senatus populusque Romanus* - the Senate and People of Rome) and stands for *Senatus populusque Lubecensis*. It was, however, affixed only in 1871. There was previously no inscription at this location. It would also have been pointless, since the view of the lower parts of the Holsten Gate from the city side was obscured by high walls.

There is another inscription on the field side. The text is "*concordia domi foris pax*" ("harmony within, peace without"). This inscription is also from 1871 and is a shortened form of the text which had previously been on the (not preserved) foregate. "*Concordia domi et pax foris sane res est omnium pulcherrima*" ("Harmony within and peace without are indeed the greatest good of all"; see "Outer Holsten Gate" below).

Fortifications on the field side [edit]

Functionally, the field and the city side have very different designs. While the city side is richly decorated with windows, this would be inappropriate on the field side considering the possibility of combat situations. On the field side there are accordingly only a few small windows. In addition, the walls are interspersed with

Figure 1: First few paragraphs of the *Holstentor* article. Colour highlighting added for illustrating (approximate) text-image correspondences. Best viewed in colour.

This is completely different in the following paragraph which provides a detailed description of the building's appearance and is accompanied by a second image. The second image is visually very similar to the first: it shows the building in its entirety, but from a different perspective. The two opposing perspectives are explicitly referenced and explained in the *appearance* section, which even uses the same phrasing as the image captions. This paragraph also mentions parts of the gate, such as the *conical roofs*, which are shown in both images.

The first subsection of the *appearance* paragraph contains a third image that is spatially aligned with it. This subsection talks about the passageway; the image shows part (of one side) of it. Note that the caption refers to the inscription, which is located in the center of the aforementioned image. This inscription is first mentioned in the paragraph that is aligned with the image. Furthermore, the entire first paragraph *passageway* lists features of the building that are no longer visible in the contemporary photographs. The second paragraph talks about the other side of the gate, which is not pictured. The most relevant reference to the image of the passageway is contained in the final paragraph which describes its inscription in detail.

In sum, this example document shows (among other things) that discourse fragments of very different size (paragraph, sentences, sentence parts, noun phrases) can refer to images as well as their regions, in a way that can be difficult to disentangle.

2.2 Semantic Types of Referential Relations

While in the previous Section 2.1, we showed different cases for *what* text fragments can relate to an image, we now discuss examples for *how* these images relate to the text. In our qualitative case study on buildings, we observed 4 frequent relations - *generic* (view of the building), *related entity, detail/part and event.*, discussed below. This classification of relation types is not empirically validated and probably far from complete, but we intend to show that there are semantically very distinct types, even in the highly restricted building domain.

Generic Generic images show the general appearance of the building and lack a concrete reference to a specific part of the text, as, for instance, the first image in Fig. 1. These images appear at various points in the document and often contain the year the image was created in their caption. In most cases, they are arranged in chronological fashion, as in Fig. 2a[1].

Related Entity Images of related entities show people (or rarely, other buildings) that are relevant to the history of the building under discussion in the article. The entity depicted in the picture is almost always explicitly referenced in the article. For example, Fig. 2b has a named individual that is named in both the caption and article.

Part or Detail Images of the *parts* type show parts or details of the entity in question. This is the most diverse category in terms of the content of the images themselves. What is depicted can range from small details like plaques to major parts of the buildings like a tower, see Fig. 1. In some cases, these parts are not physically part of the building itself, but instead something that is permanently at the same location (e.g. an *organ* in a church).

Event Images in our building domain can also depict an *event* that takes place at the building in question. In the example in Fig. 2c, the image portrays the event in progress, e.g. a plane flying through the *Arc de Triomphe*. There is also another, more subtle but also frequent subtype of event-related image which relates to the existence of the architectural object itself and is often linked to its (partial or complete) destruction, construction or its renovation. In these cases, images often show the aftermath of the destruction (as is the case in Fig. 2d) or the site in the process of renovation/rebuilding. This latter case is particularly challenging in terms of semantic analysis and image-text matching, because it often entails scenarios where the text refers to (parts of) buildings that are no longer present in the image. That means, a model that fully and correctly analyses this scenario would need to make the connection between the text passages talking about the building's destruction and the image of it in a ruined state. Both types of events generally have a clear reference to the article's text, though the length can vary.

Medium In addition to the image content, we observe that the original medium is highly relevant in figuring out its semantic relation. The domain of buildings is especially rich in different original media - articles contain digitized images of paintings, sketches, maps, diagrams, post cards or photographs. To a human reader, these are not only understood differently, but themselves contain information.

[1]for Fig. 2, see supplementary material

2.3 Discussion

Inutitively, the Wikipedia articles on buildings that we have discussed in this section constitute a relatively simple type of multi-modal document: each document introduces and discusses a single, depictable, main entity, both in terms of textual and visual elements. Many images have captions that refer to the image's main object. Typically, this object is also referred to explicitly (often with very similar verbiage) in the text, except the tricky case of *generic images* where it is less clear which specific discourse fragment is referentially related.[2] Moreover, the articles have a clear hierarchical structure and, most of the time, images are positioned next to the paragraph that they are related to.

Formally, however, these examples indicate that there is a lot of structural and semantic complexity found in naturally occuring text-image correspondences. A long range of questions could be asked to capture this correspondence: (i) which text spans refer to an image or image region and which do not refer? (ii) what is the size of the text span that refers to the image (i.e. paragraph, sentence, noun phrase, ...), (iii) which text spans refer to the same image?, (iv) which images refer to the same text span or entity?, (v) how does the text refer to the image?, (vi) how do caption and text relate to each other?, etc. As we will discuss below, most existing V&L task come nowhere near this complexity and, most notably, make a lot of simplications on the text analysis side.

3 Related Work in Vision & Language

Fixed Text-Image Relation Probably the most widely used image-text data in Vision & Language are so-called image captions that provide a general, neutral description of an image's content, cf. MSCOCO (Lin et al., 2014) or Flickr30k (Plummer et al., 2015) captions . Typical captions consist of a single sentence that directly refers to the image. Other work has looked at more fine-grained referential relations such as referring expressions in the

[2]They could be seen as being linked to the text as a whole, but this is not particularly informative for information extraction or similar tasks.

form of noun phrases that identify specific objects in an image (Kazemzadeh et al., 2014). Work on even more fine-grained resolution that captures object parts is relatively rare, but see (Hürlimann and Bos, 2016). A complementary trend is to use texts that are (slightly) longer than image captions, such as image paragraphs that describe the image content in a sequence of sentences (Krause et al., 2017) or dialogues that center on identifying an object in a sequence of turns (de Vries et al., 2017) or an image from a set of images (Das et al., 2017). All of these datasets are crowdsourced and target a referential task on a specific, fixed level, i.e. image-sentence, object-phrase, object-dialogue, image-dialogue. It is worth noting that, internally, many recent large-scale models in V&L process object-phrase relations while encoding image-sentence pairs (Lee et al., 2018; Anderson et al., 2018; Kottur et al., 2018; Tan and Bansal, 2019; Lu et al., 2020), combining referential relations on two different levels. None of these tasks and models, however, deal with image-text pairs where significant parts of the text have no relation to the visual content, thereby circumventing the need to identify fragments that do indeed stand in a referential relation to a given image.

Diverse Referential Relations There is some initial work on datasets and tasks that capture more varied semantic or discursive relations between image and text: Kruk et al. (2019) tag the image intent in multi-modal Twitter posts, distinguishing between intents like 'provocative', 'expressive' or 'promotive'. Their annotations assign a global label to the image which captures the relation to the text as a whole. This goes beyond literal image descriptions, but still does not capture structurally diverse referential relations. Alikhani et al. (2019) investigate text-image coherence in recipe texts that describe sequences of consecutive actions in a cooking context. Structurally, the recipe's text is already segmented, with an image aligned to each step. Alikhani et al. (2019) distinguish image-text relations with respect to which part of the action is shown and whether all entities affected by an action are visible/mentioned in the text. Both papers work on naturally occuring text, though these are still relatively short (tweets and 1-2 sentences per step respectively). Neither task faces the segmentation problem to a degree that is similar to the complex structure we encountered in multi-modal Wikipedia articles. By contrast, in our building example, the rhetorical purpose and authorial intent of each picture seems to be more or less uniform. That is, images are included to illustrate (as opposed to being provocative or expressive). Likewise, the semiotics of these images are overwhelmingly parallel to the content of the text.

Muraoka et al. (2020) work with a more coarse-grained and somewhat simplified version of the problem discussed in this paper. Their task is to correctly predict the physical alignment of images and sections in Wikipedia articles. This approach utilizes the inherent document structure[3], however our observations (see Section 2) call into question the presupposition that alignment in layout entails alignment in content. A similar text-image matching task is discussed in Hessel et al. (2019), where the authors seek to match the images in a document to the most relevant sentences in it (leaving out the captions). Their model is trained on collections of sentences and images from the same documents; or different documents, for instances of non-relatedness. This information is used at test time to estimate the individual links between the sentences and images of a given document. Hessel et al. (2019) is highly relevant to the concerns discussed in this paper because it has some success in grappling with the comparatively large amounts of text in the Wikipedia article genre.

4 Towards Multi-Modal Information Extraction

Many of the phenomena we have discussed in Section 2 have long been researched in NLP models that extract information from text only. Prominently, text-oriented NLP has long been interested in detecting and processing entities, i.e. Named Entity Recognition (NER) is a very well-known NLP task that is useful in a range of applications (Li et al., 2020). The most standard named entity categories are `person`, `location` and `organisation`, however there is a number of NER tools with varying tag sets. One way to model texts of the type illustrated in Fig. 1 would be to move towards multi-modal NER models that identify mentions of entities in a text and link them to corresponding images or image regions, cf. Asgari-Chenaghlu et al. (2020) for a similar proposal.

Event detection is another text-based NLP task that has been approached with the use of CNNs (Nguyen and Grishman, 2015) and, more recently,

[3] and consequently save on expensive manual annotation

attention mechanisms (Liu et al., 2017b). Multi-modal event detection could be useful to capture referential relations as shown in Fig. 2c. Finally, models that represent or encode relations between entities (Lin et al., 2016; Zhang et al., 2019) in a multi-modal text would be an extremely useful tool in our setting. As a step towards processing comparatively large chunks of text, *discourse segmentation* (Braud et al. (2017), Iruskieta et al. (2019)) splits documents into elementary Discourse Units. Parsing these texts as a discourse is also a topic of ongoing research (Liu et al., 2017a; Li et al., 2016).

To the best of our knowledge, research in Vision & Language has hardly been inspired by these classical, entity-centric task in text processing. This general impression is corroborated by the very comprehensive V&L survey of Mogadala et al. (2019).

5 Conclusion

In this paper, we have discussed some complexities of referential relations that arise in natually occurring multi-modal texts. Solving at least some of these requires the use of far more involved text processing techniques than is common for widespread V&L tasks such as image captioning or visual dialogue. Our domain - architectural sites - narrows this potentially sprawling problem somewhat. While every building is an entity unto itself, there are common features that are shared by large subsets. We argue that Wikipedia articles are a valuable source of raw data for multi-modal document analysis, since they constitute a genre of document that is freely available in large quantities and across languages.[4] However, it is questionable whether models that identify the type of image-text relations discussed in this paper can be developed without hand-annotated data. In terms of uitlity and intended audience, it may be worth considering work like Arnold and Tilton (2020), whose aim is to add robust, searchable annotations to existing collections of historical images. This leads the authors to develop a model that automatically labels images using image segmentation and a pre-defined ontology. We believe that moving towards such more realistic texts in V&L is interesting both from a linguistic, and from an application-oriented perspective, i.e. for multi-modal information extraction.

[4]Some tasks and datasets may also benefit from existing knowledge bases such as Wikidata (Vrandečić and Krötzsch, 2014).

Acknowledgements

This work was supported by a grant from the Federal Ministry of Education and Research (BMBF, grant No. 01UG2120A).

References

Malihe Alikhani, Sreyasi Nag Chowdhury, Gerard de Melo, and Matthew Stone. 2019. CITE: A corpus of image-text discourse relations. In *Proceedings of the 2019 Conference of the North American Chapter of the Association for Computational Linguistics: Human Language Technologies, Volume 1 (Long and Short Papers)*, pages 570–575, Minneapolis, Minnesota. Association for Computational Linguistics.

Peter Anderson, Xiaodong He, Chris Buehler, Damien Teney, Mark Johnson, Stephen Gould, and Lei Zhang. 2018. Bottom-up and top-down attention for image captioning and visual question answering. In *Proceedings of the IEEE conference on computer vision and pattern recognition*, pages 6077–6086.

Taylor Arnold and Lauren Tilton. 2020. Enriching historic photography with structured data using image region segmentation. In *Proceedings of the 1st International Workshop on Artificial Intelligence for Historical Image Enrichment and Access*, pages 1–10, Marseille, France. European Language Resources Association (ELRA).

Meysam Asgari-Chenaghlu, M. Reza Feizi-Derakhshi, Leili Farzinvash, M. A. Balafar, and Cina Motamed. 2020. A multimodal deep learning approach for named entity recognition from social media.

Chloé Braud, Ophélie Lacroix, and Anders Søgaard. 2017. Cross-lingual and cross-domain discourse segmentation of entire documents. In *Proceedings of the 55th Annual Meeting of the Association for Computational Linguistics (Volume 2: Short Papers)*, pages 237–243, Vancouver, Canada. Association for Computational Linguistics.

Abhishek Das, Satwik Kottur, José MF Moura, Stefan Lee, and Dhruv Batra. 2017. Learning cooperative visual dialog agents with deep reinforcement learning. In *Proceedings of the IEEE international conference on computer vision*, pages 2951–2960.

Judy Delin and John Bateman. 2002. Describing and critiquing multimodal documents. *Document Design*, 3:140–155.

Michel Hardy-Vallée. 2016. Text and image: a critical introduction to the visual/verbal divide by john a. bateman. *Visual Studies*, 31:366–368.

Jack Hessel, Lillian Lee, and David Mimno. 2019. Unsupervised discovery of multimodal links in multi-image, multi-sentence documents. In *Proceedings of the 2019 Conference on Empirical Methods in*

Natural Language Processing and the 9th International Joint Conference on Natural Language Processing (EMNLP-IJCNLP), pages 2034–2045, Hong Kong, China. Association for Computational Linguistics.

Manuela Hürlimann and Johan Bos. 2016. Combining lexical and spatial knowledge to predict spatial relations between objects in images. In *Proceedings of the 5th Workshop on Vision and Language*, pages 10–18.

Mikel Iruskieta, Kepa Bengoetxea, Aitziber Atutxa Salazar, and Arantza Diaz de Ilarraza. 2019. Multilingual segmentation based on neural networks and pre-trained word embeddings. In *Proceedings of the Workshop on Discourse Relation Parsing and Treebanking 2019*, pages 125–132, Minneapolis, MN. Association for Computational Linguistics.

Sahar Kazemzadeh, Vicente Ordonez, Mark Matten, and Tamara Berg. 2014. ReferItGame: Referring to objects in photographs of natural scenes. In *Proceedings of the 2014 Conference on Empirical Methods in Natural Language Processing (EMNLP)*, pages 787–798, Doha, Qatar. Association for Computational Linguistics.

Satwik Kottur, José MF Moura, Devi Parikh, Dhruv Batra, and Marcus Rohrbach. 2018. Visual coreference resolution in visual dialog using neural module networks. In *Proceedings of the European Conference on Computer Vision (ECCV)*, pages 153–169.

Jonathan Krause, Justin Johnson, Ranjay Krishna, and Li Fei-Fei. 2017. A hierarchical approach for generating descriptive image paragraphs. In *Proceedings of the IEEE conference on computer vision and pattern recognition*, pages 317–325.

Julia Kruk, Jonah Lubin, Karan Sikka, Xiao Lin, Dan Jurafsky, and Ajay Divakaran. 2019. Integrating text and image: Determining multimodal document intent in Instagram posts. In *Proceedings of the 2019 Conference on Empirical Methods in Natural Language Processing and the 9th International Joint Conference on Natural Language Processing (EMNLP-IJCNLP)*, pages 4622–4632, Hong Kong, China. Association for Computational Linguistics.

Kuang-Huei Lee, Xi Chen, Gang Hua, Houdong Hu, and Xiaodong He. 2018. Stacked cross attention for image-text matching. In *Proceedings of the European Conference on Computer Vision (ECCV)*, pages 201–216.

J. Li, A. Sun, J. Han, and C. Li. 2020. A survey on deep learning for named entity recognition. *IEEE Transactions on Knowledge and Data Engineering*, pages 1–1.

Qi Li, Tianshi Li, and Baobao Chang. 2016. Discourse parsing with attention-based hierarchical neural networks. In *Proceedings of the 2016 Conference on Empirical Methods in Natural Language Processing*, pages 362–371, Austin, Texas. Association for Computational Linguistics.

Tsung-Yi Lin, Michael Maire, Serge Belongie, James Hays, Pietro Perona, Deva Ramanan, Piotr Dollár, and C Lawrence Zitnick. 2014. Microsoft coco: Common objects in context. In *European conference on computer vision*, pages 740–755. Springer.

Yankai Lin, Shiqi Shen, Zhiyuan Liu, Huanbo Luan, and Maosong Sun. 2016. Neural relation extraction with selective attention over instances. In *Proceedings of the 54th Annual Meeting of the Association for Computational Linguistics (Volume 1: Long Papers)*, pages 2124–2133.

Frederick Liu, Han Lu, Chieh Lo, and Graham Neubig. 2017a. Learning character-level compositionality with visual features. In *Proceedings of the 55th Annual Meeting of the Association for Computational Linguistics (Volume 1: Long Papers)*, pages 2059–2068, Vancouver, Canada. Association for Computational Linguistics.

Shulin Liu, Yubo Chen, Kang Liu, and Jun Zhao. 2017b. Exploiting argument information to improve event detection via supervised attention mechanisms. In *Proceedings of the 55th Annual Meeting of the Association for Computational Linguistics (Volume 1: Long Papers)*, pages 1789–1798, Vancouver, Canada. Association for Computational Linguistics.

Jiasen Lu, Vedanuj Goswami, Marcus Rohrbach, Devi Parikh, and Stefan Lee. 2020. 12-in-1: Multi-task vision and language representation learning. In *Proceedings of the IEEE/CVF Conference on Computer Vision and Pattern Recognition*, pages 10437–10446.

Aditya Mogadala, Marimuthu Kalimuthu, and Dietrich Klakow. 2019. Trends in integration of vision and language research: A survey of tasks, datasets, and methods. *arXiv preprint arXiv:1907.09358*.

Masayasu Muraoka, Ryosuke Kohita, and Etsuko Ishii. 2020. Image position prediction in multimodal documents. In *Proceedings of the 12th Language Resources and Evaluation Conference*, pages 4265–4274, Marseille, France. European Language Resources Association.

Thien Huu Nguyen and Ralph Grishman. 2015. Event detection and domain adaptation with convolutional neural networks. In *Proceedings of the 53rd Annual Meeting of the Association for Computational Linguistics and the 7th International Joint Conference on Natural Language Processing (Volume 2: Short Papers)*, pages 365–371.

Yingwei Pan, Yehao Li, Jianjie Luo, Jun Xu, Ting Yao, and Tao Mei. 2020. Auto-captions on gif: A large-scale video-sentence dataset for vision-language pretraining. *arXiv preprint arXiv:2007.02375*.

Bryan A Plummer, Liwei Wang, Chris M Cervantes, Juan C Caicedo, Julia Hockenmaier, and Svetlana Lazebnik. 2015. Flickr30k entities: Collecting region-to-phrase correspondences for richer image-to-sentence models. In *Proceedings of the IEEE international conference on computer vision*, pages 2641–2649.

Hao Tan and Mohit Bansal. 2019. Lxmert: Learning cross-modality encoder representations from transformers. *arXiv preprint arXiv:1908.07490*.

Denny Vrandečić and Markus Krötzsch. 2014. Wikidata: a free collaborative knowledgebase. *Communications of the ACM*, 57(10):78–85.

Harm de Vries, Florian Strub, Sarath Chandar, Olivier Pietquin, Hugo Larochelle, and Aaron C. Courville. 2017. Guesswhat?! visual object discovery through multi-modal dialogue. In *Conference on Computer Vision and Pattern Recognition (CVPR)*.

Qi Wu, Damien Teney, Peng Wang, Chunhua Shen, Anthony Dick, and Anton van den Hengel. 2017. Visual question answering: A survey of methods and datasets. *Computer Vision and Image Understanding*, 163:21–40. Language in Vision.

Pengcheng Yang, Fuli Luo, Peng Chen, Lei Li, Zhiyi Yin, Xiaodong He, and Xu Sun. 2019. Knowledgeable storyteller: A commonsense-driven generative model for visual storytelling. In *Proceedings of the Twenty-Eighth International Joint Conference on Artificial Intelligence (IJCAI-19)*, pages 5356–5362.

Zhengyan Zhang, Xu Han, Zhiyuan Liu, Xin Jiang, Maosong Sun, and Qun Liu. 2019. Ernie: Enhanced language representation with informative entities. *arXiv preprint arXiv:1905.07129*.

6 Supplemental Material

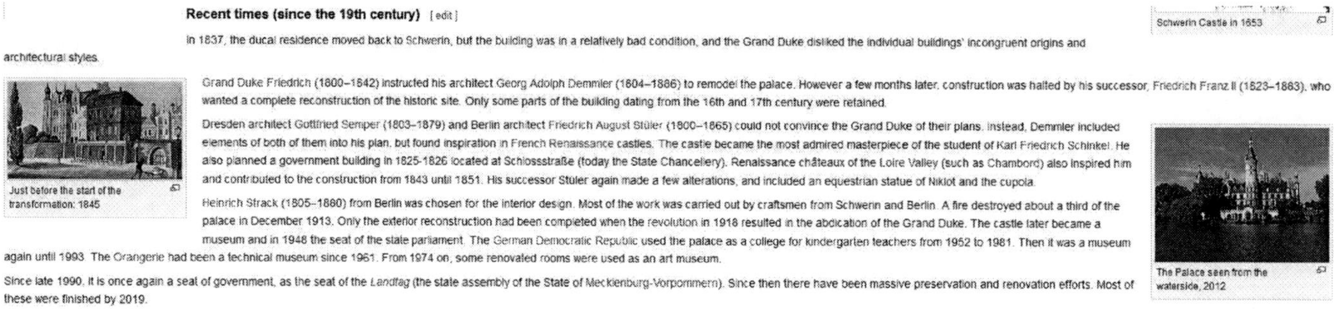
Recent times (since the 19th century) [edit]

In 1837, the ducal residence moved back to Schwerin, but the building was in a relatively bad condition, and the Grand Duke disliked the individual buildings' incongruent origins and architectural styles.

Grand Duke Friedrich (1800–1842) instructed his architect Georg Adolph Demmler (1804–1886) to remodel the palace. However a few months later, construction was halted by his successor, Friedrich Franz II (1823–1883), who wanted a complete reconstruction of the historic site. Only some parts of the building dating from the 16th and 17th century were retained.

Dresden architect Gottfried Semper (1803–1879) and Berlin architect Friedrich August Stüler (1800–1865) could not convince the Grand Duke of their plans. Instead, Demmler included elements of both of them into his plan, but found inspiration in French Renaissance castles. The castle became the most admired masterpiece of the student of Karl Friedrich Schinkel. He also planned a government building in 1825-1826 located at Schlossstraße (today the State Chancellery). Renaissance châteaux of the Loire Valley (such as Chambord) also inspired him and contributed to the construction from 1843 until 1851. His successor Stüler again made a few alterations, and included an equestrian statue of Niklot and the cupola.

Heinrich Strack (1805–1880) from Berlin was chosen for the interior design. Most of the work was carried out by craftsmen from Schwerin and Berlin. A fire destroyed about a third of the palace in December 1913. Only the exterior reconstruction had been completed when the revolution in 1918 resulted in the abdication of the Grand Duke. The castle later became a museum and in 1948 the seat of the state parliament. The German Democratic Republic used the palace as a college for kindergarten teachers from 1952 to 1981. Then it was a museum again until 1993. The Orangerie had been a technical museum since 1961. From 1974 on, some renovated rooms were used as an art museum.

Since late 1990, it is once again a seat of government, as the seat of the *Landtag* (the state assembly of the State of Mecklenburg-Vorpommern). Since then there have been massive preservation and renovation efforts. Most of these were finished by 2019.

Schwerin Castle in 1653

Just before the start of the transformation: 1845

The Palace seen from the waterside, 2012

(a) Generic: Two chronologically arranged generic images in the *Schwerin Castle* article

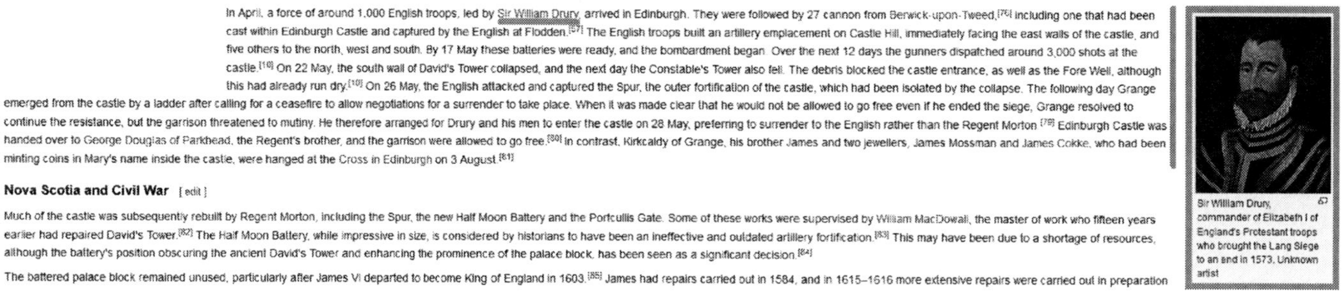
In April, a force of around 1,000 English troops, led by Sir William Drury, arrived in Edinburgh. They were followed by 27 cannon from Berwick-upon-Tweed,[76] including one that had been cast within Edinburgh Castle and captured by the English at Flodden.[77] The English troops built an artillery emplacement on Castle Hill, immediately facing the east walls of the castle, and five others to the north, west and south. By 17 May these batteries were ready, and the bombardment began. Over the next 12 days the gunners dispatched around 3,000 shots at the castle.[10] On 22 May, the south wall of David's Tower collapsed, and the next day the Constable's Tower also fell. The debris blocked the castle entrance, as well as the Fore Well, although this had already run dry.[10] On 26 May, the English attacked and captured the Spur, the outer fortification of the castle, which had been isolated by the collapse. The following day Grange emerged from the castle by a ladder after calling for a ceasefire to allow negotiations for a surrender to take place. When it was made clear that he would not be allowed to go free even if he ended the siege, Grange resolved to continue the resistance, but the garrison threatened to mutiny. He therefore arranged for Drury and his men to enter the castle on 28 May, preferring to surrender to the English rather than the Regent Morton.[79] Edinburgh Castle was handed over to George Douglas of Parkhead, the Regent's brother, and the garrison were allowed to go free.[80] In contrast, Kirkcaldy of Grange, his brother James and two jewellers, James Mossman and James Cokke, who had been minting coins in Mary's name inside the castle, were hanged at the Cross in Edinburgh on 3 August.[81]

Nova Scotia and Civil War [edit]

Much of the castle was subsequently rebuilt by Regent Morton, including the Spur, the new Half Moon Battery and the Portcullis Gate. Some of these works were supervised by William MacDowall, the master of work who fifteen years earlier had repaired David's Tower.[82] The Half Moon Battery, while impressive in size, is considered by historians to have been an ineffective and outdated artillery fortification.[83] This may have been due to a shortage of resources, although the battery's position obscuring the ancient David's Tower and enhancing the prominence of the palace block, has been seen as a significant decision.[84]

The battered palace block remained unused, particularly after James VI departed to become King of England in 1603.[85] James had repairs carried out in 1584, and in 1615–1616 more extensive repairs were carried out in preparation

Sir William Drury, commander of Elizabeth I of England's Protestant troops who brought the Lang Siege to an end in 1573. Unknown artist

(b) Related Entity: Portrait of an aristocrat in the article of *Edinburgh Castle*

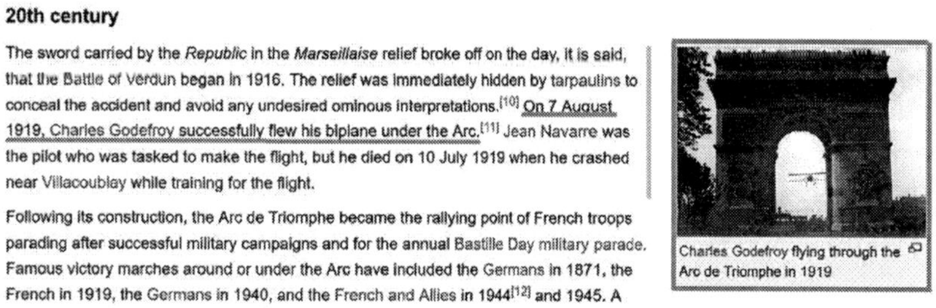
20th century

The sword carried by the *Republic* in the *Marseillaise* relief broke off on the day, it is said, that the Battle of Verdun began in 1916. The relief was immediately hidden by tarpaulins to conceal the accident and avoid any undesired ominous interpretations.[10] On 7 August 1919, Charles Godefroy successfully flew his biplane under the Arc.[11] Jean Navarre was the pilot who was tasked to make the flight, but he died on 10 July 1919 when he crashed near Villacoublay while training for the flight.

Following its construction, the Arc de Triomphe became the rallying point of French troops parading after successful military campaigns and for the annual Bastille Day military parade. Famous victory marches around or under the Arc have included the Germans in 1871, the French in 1919, the Germans in 1940, and the French and Allies in 1944[12] and 1945. A

Charles Godefroy flying through the Arc de Triomphe in 1919

(c) Event: Flight through the *Arc de Triomphe*

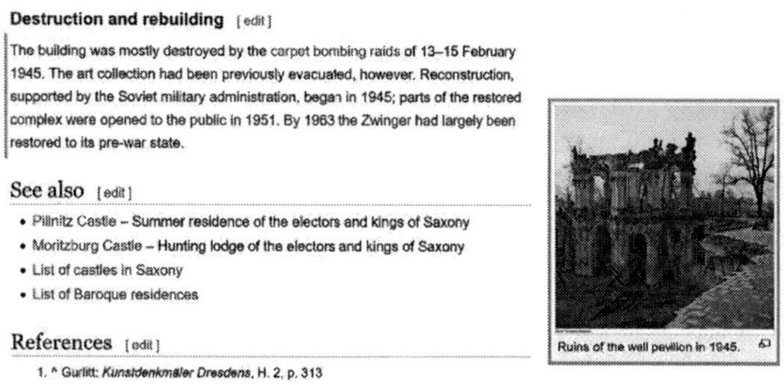
Destruction and rebuilding [edit]

The building was mostly destroyed by the carpet bombing raids of 13–15 February 1945. The art collection had been previously evacuated, however. Reconstruction, supported by the Soviet military administration, began in 1945; parts of the restored complex were opened to the public in 1951. By 1963 the Zwinger had largely been restored to its pre-war state.

See also [edit]

- Pillnitz Castle – Summer residence of the electors and kings of Saxony
- Moritzburg Castle – Hunting lodge of the electors and kings of Saxony
- List of castles in Saxony
- List of Baroque residences

References [edit]

1. ^ Gurlitt: *Kunstdenkmäler Dresdens*, H. 2, p. 313

Ruins of the wall pavilion in 1945.

(d) Event: Destruction of the *Zwinger, Dresden*

Figure 2: Examples of Semantic Referential Relations

Association for Computational Linguistics
209 N. Eighth Street
Stroudsburg, Pennsylvania 18360

ISBN 978-1-7138-2962-1

CURRAN ASSOCIATES INC.
proceedings.com